Best
TEA SHOP WALKS
IN THE
PEAK DISTRICT

Norman and June Buckley

Copyright © Norman and June Buckley, 1995

Reprinted, 1997

Published by Sigma Leisure – an imprint of
Sigma Press, 1 South Oak Lane, Wilmslow, Cheshire SK9 6AR, England.

British Library Cataloguing in Publication Data
A CIP record for this book is available from the British Library.

ISBN: 1-85058-454-0

Typesetting and Design by: Sigma Press, Wilmslow, Cheshire.

Cover: The Brookside Cafe, Wildboarclough *(Graham Beech)*

Maps: Jeremy Semmens

Photographs: the author

Printed by: Manchester Free Press

Disclaimer: the information in this book is given in good faith and is believed to be correct at the time of publication. No responsibility is accepted by either the author or publisher for errors or omissions, or for any loss or injury howsoever caused. Only you can judge your own fitness, competence and experience.

Preface

What could be more natural than the combination of walking, or should it really be rambling, generally at the easier end of the scale, with the leisurely enjoyment of traditional English refreshment in comfortable surroundings in one form or another of the ubiquitous tea shop?

In summer, the choice could well be between the refreshingly cool interior of a tea shop on the one hand, and the caressing warmth of the sun at the outside tables, on the other. In less clement weather that same interior, warm and welcoming, will form a perfect accompaniment to a walk, possibly in the rain, among good, sometimes outstanding, scenery. On such a day the toasted teacakes will never have tasted better and the added sense of achievement will surely enhance the appetite and give a virtuous glow to complement the sense of physical well-being.

The twenty-six circular walks in this book have been carefully selected to include different areas of the wonderfully varied Peak District countryside. All starting and finishing places are readily accessible from popular towns and villages and it is assumed that most walkers will use a motor vehicle for access.

The interest of the walks is enhanced by a brief description of landscape, social and industrial history, and other features where appropriate. Most of the walks are quite short but, whatever one's views of the validity of the term "Peak", this is a hilly countryside, and most circular walks will rise and fall, sometimes considerably. The summary at the beginning of the description of each walk enables a very quick assessment to be made of the time and effort likely to be required, and of the conditions underfoot.

By definition, the walks in this book are associated with tea shops, situated either along the route or at the termination. Although anchored securely on the traditional English establishment, the term "tea shop" does include a wide variety of premises serving light refreshments, ranging from one room in a cottage to the splendidly elegant ambience of Chatsworth House. Each has been assessed and found to provide, as an absolute minimum, a good pot of tea, with coffee and cold drinks as alternatives.

Food available includes scones with butter, jam and cream, cakes, and very often toasted tea cakes and/or crumpets. Many premises also provide light savoury dishes; this is mentioned where appropriate. In all cases walkers are welcome, possibly after removing boots, prices are reasonable, the premises are, at the very least, clean, wholesome, and adequately warm, crockery and cutlery are of a good standard, and service is pleasant and willing. Some tea shops will, of course, exceed these basic requirements. For example, the building may be of historic interest or have an exceptional view, or the crockery may be fine china. As with the walks, the rich diversity is part and parcel of the attraction.

Inevitably, during the quiet winter months many tea shops in country areas are open only at weekends; whilst every effort has been made to note opening days and times, it has to be recognised that proprietors will change their trading practices, often at short notice, and, indeed, that ownership and management will also change from time to time. For these reasons, telephone numbers are given.

Norman and June Buckley

Contents

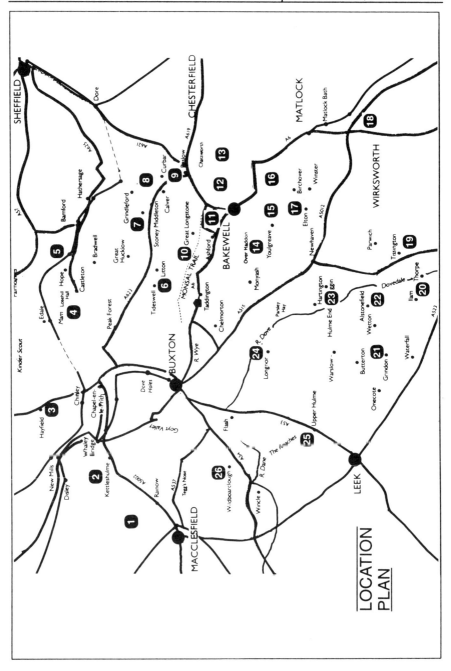

LOCATION
PLAN

Introduction

Within a comparatively small area, the Peak District offers a rich diversity of scenery, very much resulting from the underlying geology. The characteristic limestone was formed by the fusion of countless millions of minute sea creatures under the pressure of the overlying warm sea of the carboniferous period, 330 million years ago. The peaks such as Thorpe Cloud and Parkhouse Hill which occur in the limestone or "White Peak" country are the remains of reefs of harder limestone.

The limestone was then overlaid by the later formation of gritstones and shales. In most of the southern part of the district these gritstones and shales have been worn away by the elements, apart from at the extremities, notably the Staffordshire Roaches in the west and the "edges" above the Derwent Valley in the east. There are also isolated pockets of gritstone at Harthill Moor and Stanton Moor.

In the north, the gritstone cover prevails, resulting in the great moors of Kinder and Bleaklow, the "Dark Peak", with the overlying peat gouged into hags and groughs. Covered with very different vegetation, this area is much wilder and less hospitable to man than the limestone of the White Peak. Indeed, that limestone country was settled at an early stage of the history of man in Britain. Stone circles, burial mounds, and caves with human remains are all evidence of occupation for more than 4000 years. The White Peak does, however, have two very different faces. High-lying plateaux, almost flat, windswept, and tamed with difficulty for livestock farming purposes by the construction of thousands of miles of dry stone walls, the provision of dewponds, and the liberal application of the abundant lime, appear to be dominant. This not particularly attractive terrain contrasts vividly with the valleys deep cut into the limestone, often all but invisible from the adjacent plateau land above.

These sinuously winding dales, with or without rivers, constitute the Peak District feature most beloved by the numerous visitors and, inevitably, the routes for many of the best walks.

The great majority of the original afforestation of the district was progressively cleared by the early farmers. On the moors of the dark peak, which formerly had oak, elm and lime, over-grazing and burning have played the major part in the almost total loss of trees. Whilst "modern" forestry plantations such as those of the upper Derwent Valley are, at least in visual terms, a poor substitute for the original woodland, on the central and southern plateaux the numerous copses and shelter belts do soften the generally harsh landscape. Several of the limestone dales have a good variety of broad-leafed species, in some cases including the remains of ancient woodland. Nature conservation reserves have been established in appropriate places.

In 1951 the majority of this fascinating area became Britain's first National Park, a very necessary protection for a vulnerable area so close to so many conurbations. Unlike most National Parks, the Peak District has long suffered from the continuing effects of large scale extractive industries as its limestone and mineral deposits have proved to be profitable commodities. Quarrying, hacking away at the very heart substance of the countryside has, over a comparatively short period, had a more destructive effect on the landscape than many centuries of the traditional mining for lead and other minerals.

For obvious reasons, Buxton with its industrial environs and also the lower part of the Derwent Valley, had to be excluded from the Park. However, sites such as the works at Hope, an enormous blot on the landscape, remain within the Park, to be controlled by the Planning Authority as best they can.

Despite these imperfections, The Peak District has long been a popular destination for millions of visitors – motor tourists, cyclists, walkers, climbers and anglers. Indeed, the track along the lower part of the River Dove is claimed to be the most walked footpath in Britain. Whilst not neglecting the deservedly popular areas, this book does suggest a number of less frequented routes which, with their recommended tea shops, should give at least equal pleasure to those seeking them out.

✓ 1. Bollington, Kerridge Hill and The Macclesfield Canal

Length:	4½ miles.
Summary:	To reach the White Nancy end of Kerridge at 920 feet is a short, sharp, climb from the town. Having achieved this height right at the outset, it is level or downhill going for the remainder of this very pleasant round, the canal towpath providing an excellent return route.
Car Parking:	By roadside in Bollington, on route of walk, or in public car park 300 yards further along main road, past church. Grid reference (for the latter): 936779.
Map:	Ordnance Survey Outdoor Leisure No. 24, Peak District, White Peak area, 1:25000.

The Tea Shop

This is an interesting visit: the Coffee Shop is a small part of a fabric shop which in turn is a small part of a very large old mill. A proportion of this enormous building is used as offices and other retail outlets are planned. The cafe is spotless with beautifully made curtains in blue and yellow fabric and an original mural along the whole of one wall. The outlook is towards the canal and one can watch the boats cruising along. Sandwiches, scones, cakes, toasted teacakes, tea and coffee plus herbal teas and cold drinks are always available; the chocolate caramel shortcake is scrumptious!

The fabric shop will be of interest to those who enjoy sewing, patchwork, soft furnishings, etc.

Opening hours – 10.30am to 4.30pm all the year round, except Christmas Day. Tel. 01625 576443.

Adelphi Mill, Bollington

Description

Bollington is a small, former cotton manufacturing town, still semi-industrial but quite attractive in parts. Clarence Mill, originally a cotton mill of 1820, but now sub-let into factory, warehouse, and office units, stands massively beside the canal to the north of the town centre.

Kerridge is a fine outlying ridge of the Peak District, its position on the western fringe ensuring long views over the Cheshire Plain

The Macclesfield Canal is a navigable waterway, now part of the designated "Cheshire Ring" of linked canals. Long regarded as one of the country's most scenic waterways, this "narrow" canal was engineered by Telford, being completed in 1831, rather late in the canal age. From its junction with the Peak Forest Canal at Marple to the junction with the Trent and Mersey Canal at Hall Green, the length is approximately 26 miles. Its completion shortened the distance by water between London and the South, and Manchester, by 13 miles.

The Walk

Walk up Water Street, between terraces of neat stone houses. At a "T" junction by the Queen's Arms, turn right, uphill. The first objective, Kerridge, looms ahead. Turn left at the Red Lion towards Cow Lane. Ascend the steps on the right by a "public footpath" sign to follow a flagged path rising up Kerridge hill. The curious round stone tower at the top is named "White Nancy" but during 1995, it became Red, White, and Blue Nancy by the painting of the Union Jack on its surface. A coat of white paint might have been applied by the time of your visit but, in recent years, Nancy has been decked up both as a jolly Farmer Christmas and as a plum pudding!

At a fork keep left over a stile to continue uphill on steep grass, with a wall close on the right. Go straight across a more major track, heading for "White Nancy". The top is a fine viewpoint: on a clear day one can see for miles over the Cheshire Plain.

Follow the obvious path along the ridge, climbing over a ladder

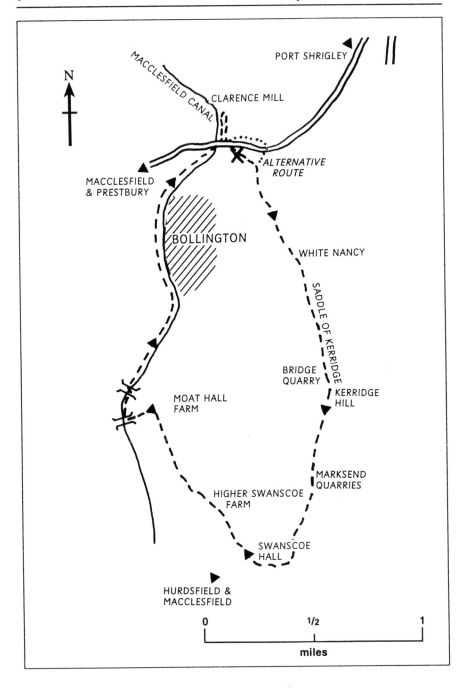

stile. Rainow can be seen, below to the left; fortunately the huge quarries to the right are rather less obvious. On reaching a minor saddle, do not rise to the peak ahead, but take a track angling down to the right. Do not take the first right fork here, but go a little further, keeping a stone wall on your right. A well-defined path descends in a straight line above disused quarries, passing the back of a house to reach the road at a junction.

Follow the road opposite, downhill, before bending right to skirt around the house and grounds of Swanscoe Hall. Fork right into a more minor road, by the entrance to the Hall. At the next fork keep right, into a cul de sac, then left in 150 yards at a "Bollington" signpost.

On reaching Shrigley Fold fork right at a footpath sign to go round the buildings. A grassy path continues to a stile and farm roadway. At a lone agricultural building, bear left to pass a rabbit warren, then a pond, keeping straight on at a gate/stile. The path is barely visible as another pond is passed, then passing between ponds at the rear of Moat Hall Farm, to reach a stile giving access to a farm lane.

Turn left towards the Macclesfield Canal, reached at bridge No. 30, which proudly displays a plaque commemorating the restoration by the Macclesfield Canal Society, unveiled by Nicholas Winterton M.P.

Turn right to follow the towpath of this attractive waterway back to Bollington, entirely tranquil despite its proximity to a fair amount of East Cheshire industry. Note the old milestones along the way. The towpath changes sides at the next bridge, which has a nicely curved horse walkway.

The Adelphi Mill, serviced by water for only the first few years of its existence, has the Barge Inn at the far end. After bridge No. 27, with a woodyard across the water, leave the towpath at a gate and turn right to descend a long, steep, flight of steps to the main road. Turn right, under the canal, then left into Clarence Road to reach the tea shop, situated on the canal side of the enormous Clarence Mill. From the tea shop, return down Clarence Road and cross the main road into Water Street to return to your car (or turn left along the main road to the car park)

2. Lyme Park

Length:	4½ miles.
Summary:	This circuit includes moorland very typical of the western fringe of the Peak District and well-varied woodland which is part of the country park surrounding Lyme Hall. As the Lyme Park moorland rises steeply from the Cheshire Plain, the walk includes a moderately strenuous ascent of about 300 feet to Dale Top. Underfoot, the route is good throughout, with just the odd muddy section.
Car Parking:	West Parkgate is reached from Poynton traffic lights by the minor road (Park Lane) heading east towards Higher Poynton, bearing right at a major fork. The line of the former railway, now the Middlewood Trail, is crossed, the road bends to the right then left, to go under the Macclesfield Canal. There are informal roadside parking places before the Methodist Church is reached. Grid reference: 948816.
Map:	Ordnance Survey, Landranger Sheet 109, Manchester and surrounding area. 1:50000.

The Tea Shop

Although the National Trust tea room at Lyme Hall serves a somewhat restricted range of food, it is still a recommended place for coffee or afternoon tea. The scones, tea, and cakes were found to be of good quality and the service was smiling.

However, plans are well-advanced for the opening of a new cafe close by the large mill pond, with more spacious surroundings and a more comprehensive menu. The present tea shop is open daily from 12 noon to 5pm from 1st April to the end of October; Saturdays and Sundays only (12noon – 4pm) until Christmas, and closed during the rest of the winter months. Tel. 01663 762023.

Lyme Hall

Description

Claimed to be the largest house in Cheshire, Lyme Hall is a stately home owned by the National Trust but financed and managed by Stockport M.D.C. It is set in beautiful and extensive grounds, now used as a country park and there have long been herds of both red and fallow deer. The house was the home of the Legh family for more than six hundred years, being largely rebuilt in the 18th century with a classical Palladian facade.

The hall and gardens are open to the public from the beginning of April to the end of September (for details tel. 01663 766492). The estate is open every day of the year from 8am until dusk. Inside the hall the attractions include Mortlake Tapestries, Grinling Gibbons carvings, and a fine collection of English clocks.

The Bow Stones, situated on the Lyme Park boundary, are thought to be of Anglo-Scandinavian origin.

The Walk

Walk up the road for a few yards to the Methodist Church and turn left along the track to Green Close Farm, passing a few houses on the way to the farm. The track goes round the back of the farm, rising steadily. More open country is reached at a farm gate

The path is always clear as it continues to rise, a little muddy underfoot, well above the valley to the left. A tiny tributary valley is crossed and, after a house has come into view, the path bends to the right across some boggy ground to a stile and gate in the wall ahead.

Turn left towards the house (Park Farm Cottage). Ignore the inviting ladder stile over the wall ahead and turn right for a slog of 300 feet or so to Dale Top, with the accompaniment of skylarks perhaps lightening the toil. Confirming the acid conditions of the gritstone moorland, great clumps of rhododendron decorate the hillside. Dale Top is a good viewpoint for Park Moor itself and with long views over the conurbation of Bramhall, Poynton, Hazel Grove and Stockport, filling the Cheshire Plain below. North of Lyme Hall the outlying "cage" tower has been visible since joining the Park Farm Cottage access roadway.

Take the left of the two stiles at the top, keeping close to the wall, slightly downhill, and then rise again to join a more major track. As a farm roadway is reached, turn left towards Bowstonegate, a dwelling which has been prominent on the skyline for some time. To the right new views have opened up from the crest of this broad ridge, including Whalley Bridge and a small part of one of the Goyt valley reservoirs.

Immediately before Bowstonegate the route goes over a stile with a "Lyme Park" signpost, making for a ladder stile with what appears to be a pets' graveyard on the right. The Bowstones are a little further along the farm roadway. From the ladder stile a well-defined path descends towards the Lyme Hall woodland and the hall itself is soon in view. The woodland is entered by bearing right at the foot of the slope to a gate and ladder stile, with a "Lyme Park" signpost.

A broad track leads ahead through the trees; fork right to head

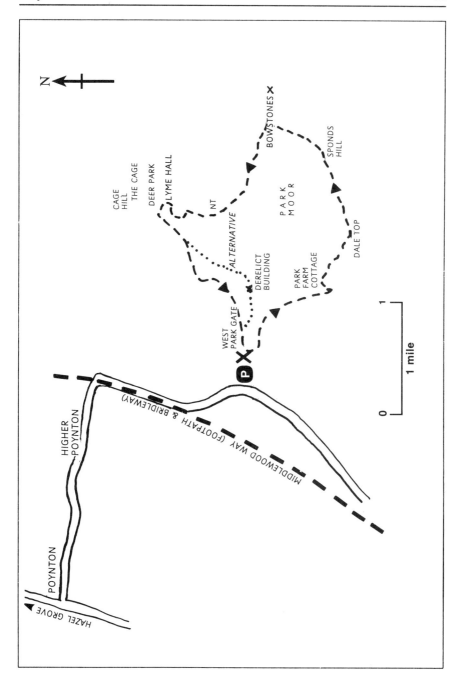

straight for the rear of the hall. The woodland contains an organised nature trail and, close to the house, is a sanctuary area where a herd of fallow deer may usually be seen. Turn left, then right to go round the house, descending a broad flight of steps to the large car park, no doubt with a feeling of virtuous superiority, having arrived by one's own efforts! Turn right again to ascend to the hall.

After suitable refreshment return to the car park below the hall, cross the stream, and take the surfaced roadway rising to the left. This provides a gentle and unmistakeable route back to West Parkgate. The road soon loses its surface and there is no through motor traffic. At a fork, keep left for the shorter route.

[If a slightly longer return on a lesser path is preferred, leave the surfaced road by forking left above a small plantation, at the crest of the rise. A faint path leads to a ladder stile and gate in the wall ahead. Don't go over this stile; turn right over another stile to take a good path rising through light woodland. Keep right, along the top of a slight ridge towards a prominent derelict building.

Bend right here to descend a well-trodden path, passing the top of a mini gritstone edge before a steep little drop to rejoin the main route to West Parkgate].

There is the unmistakeably garlic smell of ransoms by the trackside before West Parkgate is reached. The gate is locked at 6pm daily. Turn left, cross the stream, then turn right along an artificial footpath back to the car park.

3. Hayfield and The Sett Valley Trail

Length:	4 miles.
Summary:	An up and down ramble on the western fringe of the National Park, including the slopes of the hill known as Chinley Churn, with a return to Hayfield along the Sett Valley Trail, the trackbed of the former railway line serving Hayfield. Apart from a little potentially muddy ground, good underfoot.
Car Parking:	Car park situated along the Kinder Road, almost one mile from Hayfield village centre. Grid reference: 047868.
Map:	Ordnance Survey Outdoor Leisure No. 1, Peak District, Dark Peak area, 1:25000.

The Tea Shop

The proprietress of the pleasant Twenty Trees cafe is a local parish councillor with a particular interest in footpaths and access to the countryside. As would be expected, walkers are particularly welcome here.

A full menu is served throughout the day, including vegetarian food. Soup, scones, and cakes are all home-made.

Plain wood floor and tables, painted chairs, and vases of artificial sunflowers contribute to a bright, cheerful decor. A selection of daily newspapers is available for customers.

The opening hours in summer are from 10am to 5pm (closed on Monday and Tuesday). Winter – 10am to 3.30pm (closed Monday, Tuesday, and Wednesday). Tel. 01663 743213.

Description

As a former partially industrial settlement, the village of Hayfield is excluded from the National Park. It is, however, quite attractive in its rather dour, gritstone, appearance, and has long been the springboard for walks, both legal and otherwise, over the vast moorland plateau of Kinder Scout, the "Peak" itself, rising to a summit of 633m (2088 feet). The famous Kinder Trespass of the 1930s started here.

Opened in 1868 as the Marple, New Mills, and Hayfield Junction line, the single track branch railway, with services from Manchester via either Hyde or Bredbury, carried generations of walkers to this most useful railhead. Until nationalisation the line remained in joint ownership, latterly of the L.M.S. and L.N.E.R. Even well after World War II, passenger services were hauled by busy little C13/C14 tank locomotives of Great Central origin. Unfortunately, the line closed in 1970 and the trackbed later became the Sett Valley Trail.

Hayfield

The Walk

Cross the bridge over the River Kinder, towards the public conveniences and turn right to follow a signposted footpath along the side of the camping/caravan site. As might be expected in this gritstone area of the Peak District, there are masses of rhododendrons by the waterside. Pass the administrative building of the site and turn left at a junction of footpaths. Cross the site roadway by two gates and ascend a short flight of steps.

The path slants right, uphill, through the woodland to a stone stile. Go over, cross a more used path, and continue rising on a reasonably distinct path. At the top of the wood, cross the wall by a stile. Hayfield lies below, whilst behind there is a good view to the dark, brooding, mass of the Kinder Scout plateau, at 636m (2088 feet) the ultimate "peak" of the Peak District. The more modest height of Chinley Churn is straight ahead.

Head for a farm gate and stile and descend towards Stubbs Farm, keeping to the farm roadway as it twists and turns to reach the Highgate Road opposite Highgate Farm. Turn left for 20 yards, then turn right at a stile signposted "Chapel en le Frith road". Follow the line of the fence to a stile, then go down a grassy lane to the main road.

Go straight across to a signpost and descend by the stone wall. This part of the route is not well-defined, but bend left before the stream in the bottom, crossed about 150 yards lower down, then rise diagonally across a large field to a stile situated about 60 yards above an obvious farm gate. Join the trackway which links Newhouse Farm and Far Phoside, turning right.

At Far Phoside the right of way goes from gate to gate through the yard to the left of the house. But, "Beware of the dog" notices adorn each gate. Make your own decision! If you decide to play safe, go to the right before the house, keep close to the field boundary, descend a little to a farm gate, and turn sharp left up the edge of the next field to a gate which gives direct access to the desired footpath. The extra distance is negligible.

At Far Phoside turn right along a level path. Lantern Pike is the

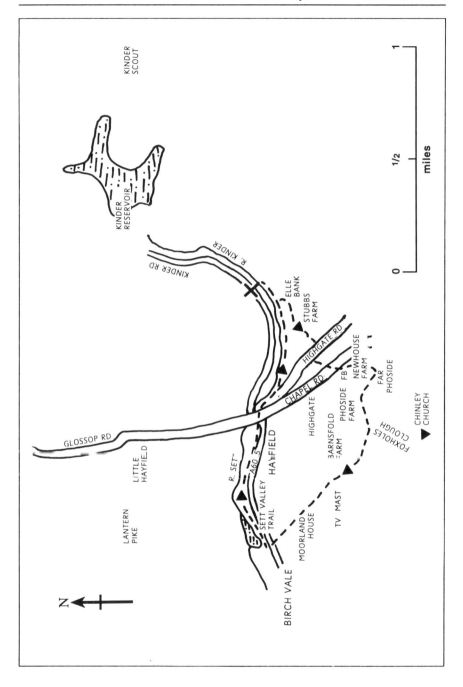

hill prominent ahead. On approaching a small wooded valley, fork left through a gate, soon turning right to cross the stream with its rapids and mini waterfalls, then left to continue the same general line. A well-used track rises quite steeply, waymarked by blue arrows, reaching its summit at about 350m (1149 ft), above Barnsfield Farm, and with extensive views.

A broad stony track descends gently towards the Sett valley, soon joining a roadway from the adjacent "TV station" [A right turn here provides a short cut back to Hayfield].

Continue along a straight lane to the main road at the Grouse Inn, close to Birch Vale. Go across the road to a path which joins the Sett Valley Trail, the trackbed of the former railway line, in a few yards. Turn right to return to Hayfield along this pleasant trail.

The trail ends at the site of the former Hayfield station, now an extensive car park with information centre and public conveniences. Note the plaque commemorating 100 years (in 1994) of the Peak and Northern Footpaths Society (formerly Peak District and Northern Counties Footpath Preservation Society), which has long played an important role in looking after walkers' interests.

Cross the main road to the church and tea shop opposite. From the tea shop turn left, uphill, take the first left turn, then left again immediately. Across the road at this junction is the former Co-operative Society store, dated 1871 and with an interesting plaque over the double door. Follow Valley Road. At a signpost keep left towards "Kinder via reservoir". A well-made track, sandwiched between the river and the camping/caravan site, rejoins the outward route for the last section to the car park.

4. Castleton

Length:	4 miles.
Summary:	A comparatively gentle walk around the head of the valley allows full appreciation of both the lovely setting and the geological interest of what is undoubtedly one of the District's finest villages.
Car Parking:	Public car park close to Speedwell Cavern, but entered from the former Mam Tor road. Grid reference: 140828.
Map:	Ordnance Survey Outdoor Leisure No. 1, Peak District, Dark Peak area. 1:25000.

The Tea Shop

Rose Cottage is by the side of the main road in Castleton but don't let that deter you. Inside, the cottage is beamed, with dark Windsor backed chairs and matching tables, whilst at the rear is a delightful patio tea garden for sunny days – so whatever the weather it is a good place for refreshment when most of the walk has been completed. Walkers are welcomed but, as the cafe is carpeted, muddy boot removal is advisable.

The blackboard chalked menu ranges from cooked meals to chilled orange juice and includes all the expected components of afternoon tea. Sandwiches are freshly made to order and are attractively served with salad garnish.

Opening hours are from 10am to 5pm daily, but closed on Fridays. From early January to late February, open Saturdays and Sundays only. Tel. 01433 620472.

Description

The four sets of limestone caverns open to visitors are only one of the reasons why Castleton is one of the Peak District's most popular centres. The situation at the foot of the great scarp crowned by the remains of Peveril Castle, built by King Henry II in 1176, is superb.

So close to the northern limestone/gritstone divide (the "White" and "Dark" Peaks), the area has been described as an "open air geology classroom". Although a great deal of lead, and some silver, were mined for centuries, the most famous mineral now is the comparatively rare "Blue John", found predominantly in the mine of the same name. Each of the other sets of caverns has its own special appeal: Treak Cliff has superb stalactites; Peak Cavern has its immense entrance and the former rope making industry inside the cave; Speedwell has access by boat.

The former Odin Mine (not open to visitors) is one of the oldest in the district although claims of Saxon origin and naming are rather dubious. Across the road from the mine entrance are a lead crushing ring and millstone. The stone was pulled round by a horse.

Remains at Odin Mine and Mam Tor

The close-knit village itself is an attractive jumble of buildings around a church much restored in 1837, but still having a Norman arch behind the pulpit and box pews. A small local history museum was founded in 1986, occupying the former schoolroom of the Methodist church. Opening hours are rather limited and the museum is closed altogether in winter; enquiries may be made by telephoning 01433 621622.

Shops, inns, accommodation including a youth hostel, and cafes, are plentiful in Castleton.

The Walk

Cross the road by the car park entrance and turn right. In less than 100 yards turn left into a lane, soon forking left. To the left is the great gash of the Winnats Pass and ahead on the hillside are the buildings marking the entrance to the Treak Cliff series of caverns. In this area the chattering of school field studies parties far exceeds the more harmonious noise made by the numerous birds.

By the entrance to Knowlgates Farm (old millstone in yard), turn left to go over two stiles and follow a rising grassy path heading towards the impressive face of Mam Tor, through a National Trust Woodland Conservation Area. The disturbed ground hereabouts is evidence of long abandoned industrial activity, confirmed when the site of the former Odin Mine, with displayed millstone, is reached. Across the road is an accessible mine entrance.

To carry on, walk up the road, closed to all except farm traffic since 1979. An information board gives an outline history of the geology of this most unusual area and of the attempts to maintain a usable road over the years. It is chastening to realise that, in this era of high technology, the "shivering mountain" won in the end and the A625 was eventually closed, leaving Castleton without an adequate approach road from the west. A little way further along the way, some remaining road surface provides wonderful evidence of what nature can do to a modern asphalt roadway.

As the road does a left bend, turn right into the stony approach roadway to Mam Farm. Go left round the back of the farm. By Tor

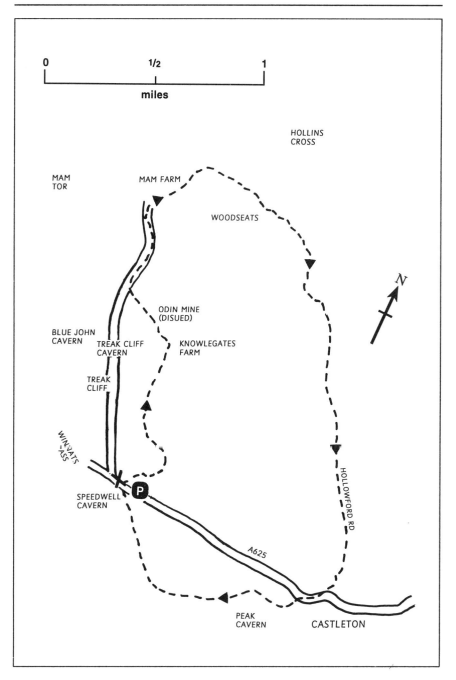

House, descend a little to the right to a farm gate. Go through the gate and straight ahead. The path is not marked on the ground, but cross the field keeping roughly the same distance from the wall on its left boundary. Woodseats Farm is below, well to the right of the route.

At the far corner of the field the stile is almost concealed behind a negotiable section of walling. Go over and bear right, to follow a minor path a few yards above the fence. Pass above Woodseats Farm, bearing gradually right to join the farm roadway at a signposted stile.

Turn left along the roadway, soon joining the Hollowford Road, which provides an easy, attractive, ramble for the remaining distance to Castleton. In the village turn right, along the main street. The recommended tea room is on the right.

Cross the road, pass the church, then the youth hostel, and turn right along a narrow road, by the fish and chip shop. Continue past the access to Peak Cavern, crossing the stream which issues from this mighty hole and ascending Gorse Hill. The road soon becomes a stony track then, on reaching open country, a good path contouring around the hillside towards the Speedwell Cavern buildings. Cross the Winnats road and bear right to return across two small fields to the car park.

5. Hope and Win Hill

Length:	4½ miles.
Summary:	A straightforward climb up and down Win Hill (462m – 1516 ft) by different routes. Good underfoot throughout, and with superb views over the upper Derwent and Hope valleys.
Car Parking:	Public car park in Hope village, adjacent to the church. Grid reference: 172835.
Map:	Ordnance Survey Outdoor Leisure No. 1, Peak District, Dark Peak area. 1:25000.

The Tea Shop

As the walk below starts and finishes just opposite the first-rate Woodbine Cafe in Hope, the self-indulgent might be tempted to stop for morning coffee before departure and then relax with afternoon tea on return. For the seriously hungry, campers' and vegetarian breakfasts are available.

Pine tables and benches, with an open fire in winter, set the tone for the cosy interior, whilst on sunny days the small, sheltered, terrace at the rear is appealing.

The choice of sandwiches includes toasted black pudding, with a good selection of scones, cakes, and beverages. Vegetarian dishes are on the menu and even gluten-free food is available on request. Tea and coffee may be purchased by the pot or by the pint!

Opening hours are 8.30am to 5pm (sometimes later) daily throughout the year. Tel. 01433 621407.

Description

Win Hill, with its attractively rocky little top, is a celebrated view-

point and is not
in any way diffi-
cult to climb. It
is certainly a
place to linger
on a clear day.

Whilst Hope
would never
win any compe-
tition for the
prettiest village
in Derbyshire, it
is not entirely
without interest.
The village was
an important
trading centre in
medieval times,
and the church
is the only one
in the extensive
area covered by
the former Royal
Forest of the
Peak to be men-
tioned in the
Domesday
Book. A Saxon
cross stands in
the churchyard.

Aston Hall, in
private owner-
ship, was built
in the 16th cen-
tury.

Shaft of Saxon Cross, Hope churchyard

The Walk

Turn right along the main road towards Sheffield. Just after the speed derestriction sign and across the bridge over the River Noe, turn left into Aston Lane. Win Hill, the principal objective of the walk, can be seen ahead; away to the left is the graceful shape of Lose Hill.

Go under the railway line and continue along this pleasant lane, rising all the way to Aston hamlet. Pass a road junction and, before the last group of buildings on the left, turn left by a cattle drinking trough. A well-worn grassy footpath rises attractively towards Win Hill. The path becomes less obvious as it crosses a large meadow to a stile in the top wall. The correct line is just to the left of some hawthorns which are probably the remains of an outgrown hedge.

After the stile the landscape changes abruptly to heather moorland, the still rising path initially following a shallow depression. The famous Win Hill views now begin to open up, including a glimpse of part of Ladybower reservoir. Ignore paths to left and right but, on approaching the huge and rather dull forestry plantation, go either right or left at a fork. Enter the woodland and turn left uphill to reach the attractively rocky summit of the hill, at a height of 462m (1516 ft).

Assuming the day is clear, time is well-spent here, admiring the fine mixture of hill, woodland and water. The prominence of Lose Hill brings to mind the (unlikely?) story that Edwin, King of Northumbria made his camp on Win Hill prior to fighting a battle in the nearby Hope valley. His defeated opponent camped on Lose Hill, opposite, hence the names of the two hills.

To return to Hope, continue over the summit, fork left at a large cairn, and descend to reach farming land at a stile with yellow arrow. Follow the direction of the arrow and carry on down to Twitchill Farm, the last section being on steep grass. Go through the farm and follow the access roadway as far as the railway line. Those with an eye for such things will notice that there are still operational sidings here, serving the enormous works of which the chimney has been so prominent ahead. Go right and then left to pass under the railway,

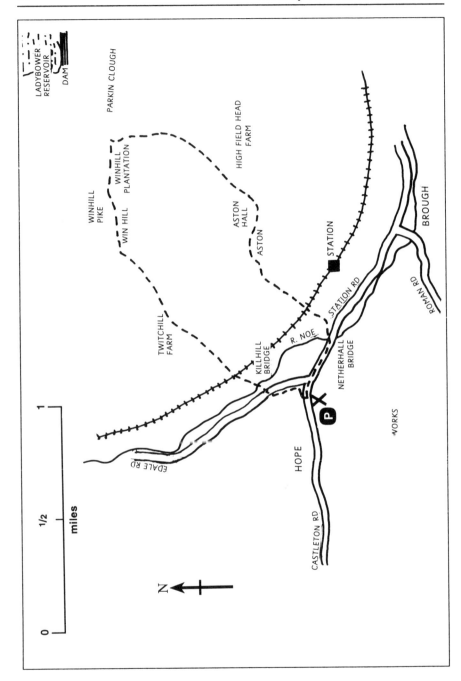

then along the lane leading to the Edale road, crossing the River Noe on the way.

Cross the road to a squeezer stile, turn left in 100 yards or so, opposite a "Losehill" signpost, and pass between houses and school. Continue along a housing estate road, bear left to a gate and surfaced footpath at the rear of Shirley Close, soon reaching the main road. The Woodbine Cafe is 30 yards to the right and the car park is opposite.

The Woodbine cafe, Hope

6. *Tideswell and Miller's Dale*

Length:	6¼ miles
Summary:	Tideswell Dale, Miller's Dale, Monk's Dale, and upland farming country combine to make a fine circular walk, with the only serious ascent on the lane rising from Monk's Dale. This latter dale contains a National Nature Reserve, approximately 100 species of flowering plant being recorded here. However, most of the path along Monk's Dale is hard going, muddy, stony, and generally slippery. If pleasant easy walking outweighs botanical interest, then the suggested alternative to Monk's Dale will probably be preferred.
Car Parking:	Small official car park with picnic area and public conveniences less than 1 mile south of Tideswell on the road leading to Miller's Dale. Grid reference: 154743.
Map:	Ordnance Survey Outdoor Leisure No. 24, Peak District, White Peak area. 1:25000.

The Tea Shop

The Hills 'n' Dales tea and craft shop on the main street serves morning coffee, light lunches, and afternoon tea, all in pleasant surroundings, enhanced by a good display of greetings cards and small craft items.

The range includes home-made soup, sandwiches, filled jacket potatoes, scones, cakes, Derbyshire cream teas, and quite a rarity these days, milk shakes!

Opening hours are from 10am to 4pm (until 5pm on Saturdays and Sundays), Wednesday to Sunday each week. Tel. 01298 871519

Cottages at Tideswell

Description

Tideswell is a large village situated at an altitude of 900 feet on the central plateau area of the white, limestone, Peak District.

Despite having declined somewhat from its more important days as a centre of the lead and wool trades, with market charter, the village still has a surprisingly good range of shops and some very attractive buildings. Paramount is the 14th century church of St. John the Baptist, the so-called Cathedral of the Peak, evidence of Tideswell's importance at that time. Large, light, and airy, it is full of interesting things including comparatively modern wood carvings by a local craftsman, Advent Hunstone.

Miller's Dale hamlet is attractively situated at the junction of Miller's Dale and Monk's Dale, close to the double viaduct which carried the Midland Railway main line from Manchester to Derby high over the valley road and the River Wye. The remains of a mill water wheel are visible, close to the inn.

Monk's Dale is managed by English Nature, with flower rich pastures and the preservation of some ancient wild woodland, including coppicing of the hazel at 15 year intervals. This encourages both the growth of rare plants and the presence of butterflies and other wildlife.

The Walk

Leave the car park by a broad, well-made, track beside the public conveniences, descending gently down Tideswell Dale. At a fork by a bridge over the stream, either path may be followed as they soon re-join. Exposed limestone rock faces and a few minor caves/tunnels add interest to this entirely pleasant walk along the dale.

Turn left as a surfaced road is reached by a car parking area, soon reaching Litton Mill, a large mill in a small village, squeezed by the side of the Wye within the tight confines of Miller's Dale. Opposite the far end of the long terrace of cottages, turn right at a signpost to a footbridge which crosses both the river and the broad leat which channelled great quantities of water to power the machinery at Litton Mill.

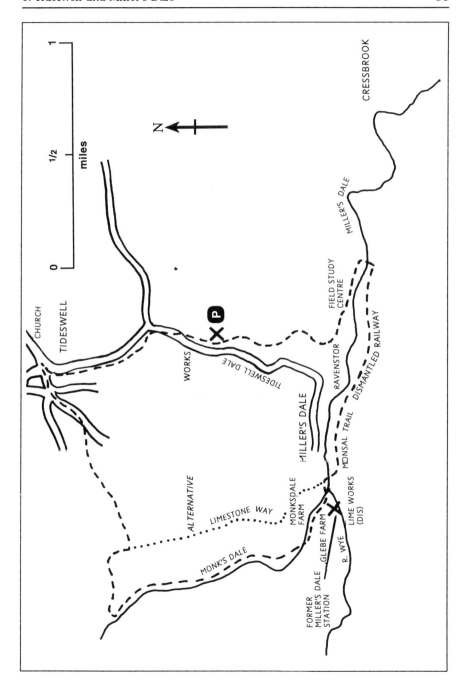

Ascend the far bank to join the Monsal Trail, the former railway line, more fully described in Walk 10. Turn right under a bridge to follow the trail. As would be expected, the former trackbed is excellent underfoot. Across the narrow valley the great rock face of Ravenstor, beloved of generations of rock climbers, can be seen through the trees as progress is made towards Miller's Dale.

As the hamlet comes into view, turn right on to a minor path descending steeply to reach a footbridge over the river and the valley road.

[To visit the former Miller's Dale station, now providing a large car park and public conveniences, stay with the trail over the viaduct, turn right at the station, and follow the road towards Glebe Farm. Immediately before the farm turn right at a signpost and descend to join the main route behind the church].

From Miller's Dale, Monk's Dale is entered by a path rising behind the tiny Victorian church, so steep that you can look down on the church tower. [The Monk's Dale avoiding route follows a lane which is designated as the "Limestone Way" rising from Miller's Dale hamlet via Monk's Dale Farm on the hillside above. The lane then reaches the plateau and runs parallel to Monk's Dale. The right turn to return to Tideswell is at the signpost mentioned under the main route]. There is no route finding problem in Monk's Dale, but be sure to keep right at a point near the start where yellow-headed stakes in the ground head left up the hillside. Apart from one clear section, the dale as a whole is well-wooded

At the top of the dale a rough meadow is crossed to join a minor road at a stile. Turn right to ascend the side of the dale, emerging into open countryside. Opposite a lone house turn right into a lane signposted "Limestone Way". In about 300 yards turn left over a stile with a "Tideswell" signpost. The path leads back to the village, crossing a series of close-cropped meadows, not always very distinct on the ground, but keeping a fairly straight line from stile to stile and parallel with the nearby road.

As the field walls close in, a stile by a farm gate gives access to a lane. Bear left to a road at the edge of the village. The way to the centre and the Hills 'n Dales tea shop is now obvious.

From the tea shop continue down the main street, forking right just after the Horse and Jockey inn. Follow a back street for 400 yards and cross a minor road to a signpost "public footpath, Tideswell Dale". Carry on through a rather messy semi-industrial area for 100 yards and follow a broad, easy, track as far as a stile by a farm gate. Go over the stile and descend a narrower path to join the road by the "Water Reclamation" (sewage) works. In 250 yards cross the road to take a track by a line of mature trees, leading directly to the car park.

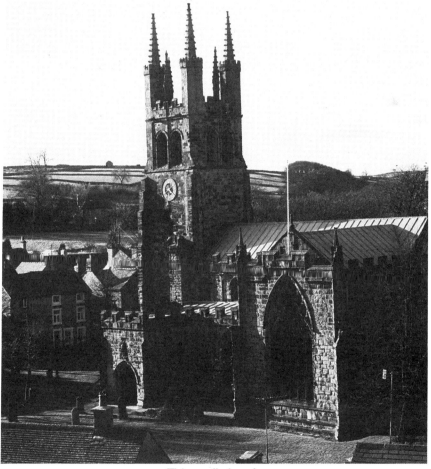

Tideswell church

7. *Foolow and Eyam*

Length:	5 miles
Summary:	A very easy, almost level, walk across part of the Peak District central plateau, starting and finishing at the charming village of Foolow and visiting Eyam, a village with absorbing and poignant history.
Car Parking:	Roadside spaces in Foolow village. Grid reference: 191768.
Map:	Ordnance Survey, Outdoor Leisure No. 24, Peak District, White Peak area. 1:25000.

The Tea Shop

Understandably, the popular village of Eyam is not short of places to eat. We enjoyed a good afternoon tea at The Eyam Tea Rooms, situated in the Square, at the far end of the village. Lots of old world charm, including waitresses in long skirts and aprons, and tableware of a pleasing design. The building itself dates from 1631 and was the "Bold Rodney Inn" until 1901, when it first become used as tea rooms.

Tea or coffee are accompanied by a good choice of scones and cakes, whilst home-made soup, salads, and sandwiches are available for those with an appetite.

Open daily (but closed on Mondays except Bank Holidays) from 10 30 – 5pm Easter to September, and open only on Saturdays and Sundays during February, March, April, and October. Closed November, December, and January. Tel. 01433 631 274

Description

Eyam is known throughout the world for the suffering of its population during the 17th century great bubonic plague outbreak, when infection carried by chance in a box of clothes sent from London to a tailor lodging in the village spread rapidly and fatally. Led by the Rector, William Mompesson, and his predecessor, Thomas Stanley, the villagers voluntarily isolated themselves from any contact with the outside world in an endeavour to prevent further spread of infection. Between 1665 and 1666, 259 of the population of about 350 died, including Mompesson's wife Katherine.

There are still many sad memorials of this great sacrifice to be seen in and around Eyam, including the cottage where the outbreak started, several sets of family graves, and "Cuckett Delf" south of the village where services were held in the open air as it was feared that congregating in the church would increase the risk of infection. Mompesson's Well, best known of the places where goods and messages were left and washed coins placed in payment, is about ½ mile along the minor road leaving the village to the north.

The church of St. Lawrence has an 8th century Celtic cross, evidence of early Christian worship in Eyam. The present church, probably the third on the site, largely dates from about 1350. Mompesson's carved oak chair, rescued from a Liverpool antique dealer, has been preserved in the church.

Ancient cross in Eyam churchyard

Also in Eyam is the Hall, a 17th century manor house open to the public for guided tours from Easter to the end of October, on Wednesdays, Thursdays, Sundays, and Bank Holiday Mondays. A small museum close to the village car park has a detailed description of the plague among its local history collection.

Of the village's subsequent growth and prosperity as an industrial settlement – lead, cotton, silk and shoes – there is now little evidence, although Hall Hill troughs which helped to provide the very early public water supply can still be seen.

Foolow appears to have had a relatively untroubled history, but with green, 14th century cross, and duckpond at its centre it is undoubtedly one of the Peak District's prettiest villages.

The Walk

Start along the road towards Housley and the main road. Some way along this road is a layby which could be used to avoid parking in Foolow. Bear left at a road fork and, just before the main road, turn left into a stony lane, unsuitable for motors.

The lane dips and then rises in crossing a small depression, rather grandly named as "Linen Dale", continuing between countless stone walls towards Eyam. Keep straight on at any junction. At the edge of Eyam, pass Fairview Farm, the lane now becoming Tideswell Lane and descending to join a more major road at Town Head. Turn right to reach the main part of the village.

No particular route is set within Eyam. With the exception of some of the family graves and Mompesson's Well, all the interesting features can readily be visited in or close to the main built-up area The tea shop is at the far end, just beyond the junction which brings the road through Eyam Dale to the village.

From the tea shop, return through the village and turn left into Tideswell Lane. Close to this junction are the Town Head factory, with a plaque, and the former 17th century Townhead Inn.

Follow Tideswell Lane and, just before the top of the rise, look very carefully for old stone steps and a footpath sign on the right.

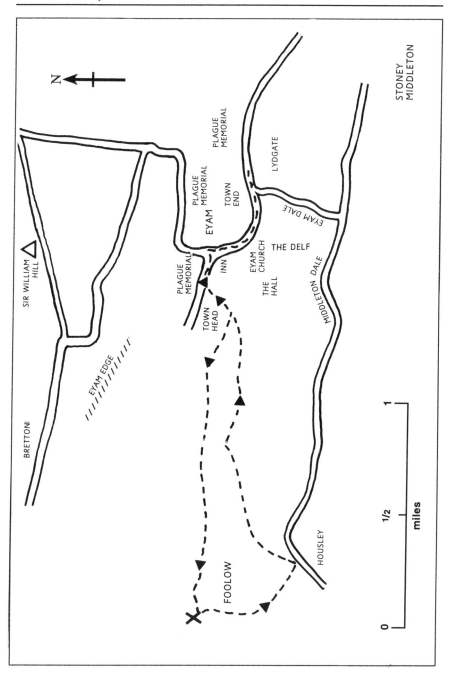

Take this footpath which provides a well-defined and generally level grassy route across the fields in a fairly straight line to Foolow. Stiles come in several shapes and sizes and some of the numerous limestone walls are broken down.

Prominent below Eyam Edge on the right is the Black Hole Mine Works. More attractively, Foolow village is in view ahead for much of the way. Just short of the village, there is a choice of path at an old finger post. Either will suffice; the right fork to join a minor road is the more straightforward.

Plague cottages, Eyam

8. Froggatt and Calver

Length:	2¼ miles.
Summary:	Without doubt this is the easiest walk in the book, an entirely gentle ramble by the side of the River Derwent without any ascent or difficulty underfoot.
Car Parking:	With care, a few roadside spaces may be found in Froggatt, quite close to the bridge. Grid reference: 244762.
Map:	Ordnance Survey, Outdoor Leisure No. 24, Peak District, White Peak area, 1:25000

The Tea Shop

The Eating House at the Derbyshire Craft Centre at Calver Bridge is, not surprisingly, a popular place and can become quite crowded at times. Everything, including some vegetarian meals such as cauliflower and broccoli cake and nut loaf, is made on the premises. Scones, cakes and tea were all found to be excellent, the decor pleasant, and the service friendly.

The tea room is open from 10am to 5.30pm daily except for the middle two weeks in January, when it is open only on Saturdays and Sundays. Tel. 01433 631583.

Description

Froggatt is a quiet, pleasantly unassuming village beautifully situated below Froggatt Edge, probably the best known of the gritstone scarps which dominate the eastern rim of the Derwent valley. The oddly arched 17th century packhorse bridge over the river is sufficiently wide for modern vehicular traffic.

The centre and bulk of Calver village lie to the south-west of the main A623 road. This circuit avoids crossing that road, staying on

Froggatt Bridge

the north-east side, where the craft shop, tea room, and mighty Calver Mill are situated. The mill was built for cotton spinning and the large quantities of water required to provide the power were brought from the great weir half a mile upstream, along the channel known as The Goit.

The Walk

Cross Froggatt Bridge and turn left immediately to take a broad riverside path among the conifers. A little further on there is a wetland area to the right of the path, with large numbers of distressed trees struggling to cope with the adverse conditions. Because of the mill weir ahead, the river is broad and tranquil.

Cross Stoke Brook by the footbridge and continue to New Bridge, crossed by the Froggatt to Calver road. Go straight across into a broad track passing in front of bungalows. To the left is the weir which provided a head of water for the mill. The track continues along the

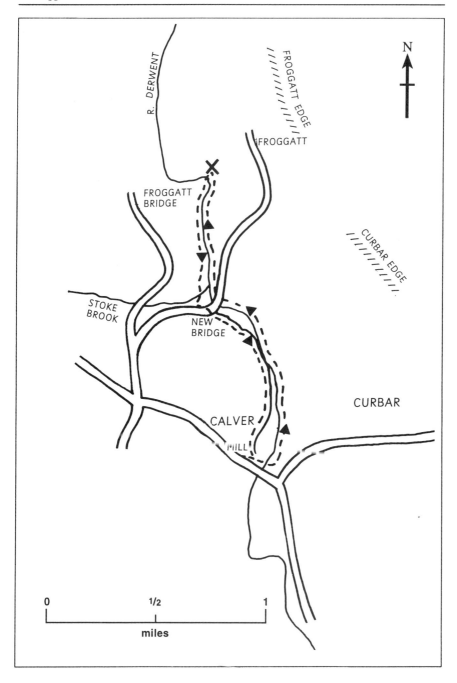

side of the feeder waterway (The "Goit"). As the mill comes into view through the trees, bear right, away from the river, across a large meadow towards Stocking Farm. The most prominent building has a redundant bell tower at one end.

The outward route is completed by passing the mill, reaching the public road, and turning right to the tea shop.

To return from the tea shop, turn left to cross the Derwent on the footbridge by the side of the old road bridge. Turn left, then left again into Duke's Drive, signposted "Froggatt 1". In a short distance, at the end of the riverside wall, take the footpath on the left, signposted "New Bridge". This path clings to the river bank as far as the bridge; the massive stone construction of the weir, now a little dilapidated, is well seen from this side of the river. The garlic scented ransoms are thick by the trackside as the bridge is approached.

Cross the road, descend the steps, and carry on along a similar riverside path, brightened by the planting of a variety of garden shrubs and daffodils along the waterside. Almost too soon Froggatt Bridge is reached along this delightful path.

9. Baslow and Curbar

Length:	3½ miles
Summary:	An easy walk along the side of the Derwent valley, below the crags of Baslow Edge, with a variation to return along the top of the Edge.
Car Parking:	Pay and Display car park by the side of the main A619 in Baslow village. Grid reference: 258721.
Map:	Ordnance Survey, Outdoor Leisure No. 24, Peak District, White Peak area. 1:25000.

The Tea Shop

The very attractive Goose Green Tea Room is situated in a popular part of Baslow. The harmonious decor includes green painted furniture, fresh flowers on the tables, and ornamental ducks. The food sampled was of good quality, with excellent tea; on request, lemon instead of milk, was willingly provided. Although there is a counter service system, table clearance and cleaning were swift and efficient in this understandably busy cafe.

Opening hours are from 9.30am to 5pm (Thursday 4pm). Closed on Fridays. Open all the year except 23rd, 24th and 25th December. Tel. 01246 583000.

Description

Baslow is a large village, which suffers from the disruptive effect of being fringed by important and busy roads. However, there are old houses and the parish church in the quieter area by the old bridge. The range of facilities and the situation in proximity to the gritstone edges and to Chatsworth Park make the village a good centre for walkers.

Baslow Edge, Curbar Edge, and Froggatt Edge form part of the

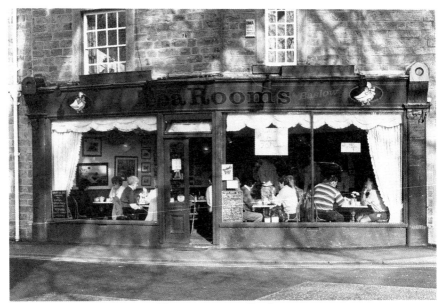

The tea room at Baslow

impressive gritstone rim which stretches for so many miles along the east side of the Derwent valley. Generations of rock climbers have learned their craft on these gullies and buttresses.

Curbar is a scattered village, mainly consisting of comparatively modern houses, climbing high on the slope below the Edge.

The Walk

Cross the main road and walk up the residential road, Eaton Hill, opposite. Turn right into Bar Road, rising steadily. The road becomes a lane, losing its surface. As it bends to the right, take a most inviting footpath on the left by a spring named "Lady Wall Well" by the Ordnance Survey.

The rising track traverses blazing yellow gorse, well above the roof tops of Baslow, the peacefulness contrasting with the hustle and bustle on the main roads flanking the village. To the right and ahead are Baslow Edge, Curbar Edge, and Froggatt Edge. The track rises for a total length of about ½ mile.

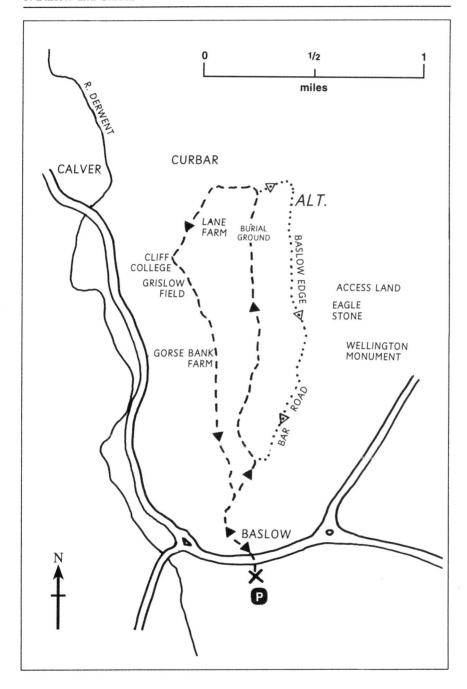

After a ladder stile, bear right along a farm type roadway, followed by a short section of walled lane. Go straight ahead to leave the farm track, with a wall close on the left and a rudimentary "footpath" sign. As the path forks, keep to the right to maintain height. Close to Curbar, the path becomes somewhat diffuse among large boulders, bracken and some swampy ground. Choose the best looking vari- · ation, always keeping straight ahead, making for a gate in the stone wall, with a notice on a post adjacent.

Bend left to a squeezer stile and descend to the road and to Curbar village.

Ignore the first signpost and stile, pass a "strictly private" lane, and turn left along the surfaced roadway leading to Lane Farm, signposted "footpath Baslow". As the farm entrance is reached, there is a curious building on the left, at first glance looking not unlike a dovecote. However, it is claimed that this building was used as a shelter for prisoners before transit to distant gaols.

Turn right to a small gate and a walled footpath descending past Lane Farm. The route is now quite clear, with the occasional "footpath" sign in places where there could be any possible doubt. A left turn and rise takes the path behind Grislow Field. The next farm is Gorse Bank; here, the path passes between the buildings. The farm roadway leads back easily to Baslow, joining Bar Road for return to the car park.

[For an alternative return route, above Curbar turn right instead of left, to take an obvious track climbing to Curbar Gap. Join the road but, in about 150 yards, turn right at a gate. Leave the main track by forking right to take the path which follows the top of the Edge back towards Baslow. Before reaching the Wellington Monument, turn right down a wide track which, in turn, becomes the lane used at the start of the walk, and then Bar Road].

10. Monsal Head and Monsal Dale

Length:	2¼ miles
Summary:	Part of the Monsal Trail on the trackbed of the former Midland Railway is combined with well-used footpaths and a short length of minor road to make this short but very attractive walk. The ascent from river level to Monsal Head is considerable but the gradient is easy and the path is good.
Car Parking:	Small public car park in the dale, close to the road junction by Upperdale Farm. Grid reference: 176722
Map:	Ordnance Survey, Outdoor Leisure No. 24 Peak District, White Peak area. 1:25000

The Tea Shop

There seem to be quite a few places around this complex to take refreshments but Monsal View Cafe and Craft Shop is the one facing the magnificent view and the famous viaduct. It is a genuine walkers' cafe. Stone floors, an open fire, and the availability of large mugs of tea or coffee all contribute to a good friendly atmosphere. Appropriately, railway memorabilia have been used in the decoration. Open daily (10.30 – 5pm) all the year round, but closed for most of January and also on Thursdays from November to March. Tel. 01629 640346

Description

The valley of the River Wye, cutting deeply through the limestone of the central plateau of the Peak District, changes its name with bewildering frequency. Near to Buxton it is Ashworth Dale then, in turn, Wye Dale, Chee Dale, Miller's Dale, Litton Dale, Water cum Jolly Dale, and Monsal Dale.

Monsal Trail from Monsal Head

The winding course of Monsal Dale is one of the most spectacular and best loved portions of this wonderful valley, arguably enhanced by the viaduct which carried the railway across the river, close to Monsal Head. Despite appearances from the dale bottom, Monsal Head is not, of course, a dale head at all but merely a mighty bluff standing 500 feet or so above the river, which winds submissively around its foot.

The Monsal Trail follows the trackbed of the former Midland Railway main line from Derby to Manchester for several miles of the valley of the Wye and, indeed, to beyond Bakewell. Like the Settle and Carlisle railway, this was an example of the Midland Railway's determination not to be thwarted by geographically difficult country. This line opened in 1867, much to the wrath of the early conservationist John Ruskin whose bitter denunciation of the despoliation of this rural paradise is quoted on a lineside notice close to the mouth of the tunnel. The line closed in 1968, the heavy puffing Jubilees and Black Fives are gone but, ironically, the now useless viaduct is preserved as a protected structure, giving pleasure to large numbers of walkers and other visitors.

Monsal Head is an outstanding viewpoint with an inn in addition to the teashop. With parking space for well over 300 cars, it becomes very crowded in high season.

The Walk

At the road junction close to the car park turn right to cross the River Wye, pass under a former railway bridge with fine skewed brickwork under its arch, and bear left to join the Monsal Trail at the site of the old Monsal Dale station. Continue along the trail towards the impressively steep Monsal Head. The river is forced to bend sharply to the right, but the railway builders refused to be diverted in the same way and tunnelled boldly through the Head for a distance of almost ⅓ mile.

On reaching the viaduct which carried the line 80 feet above the river, the route is to the right at a stile and small gate, following a muddy path down to join a better track close to the river. Before

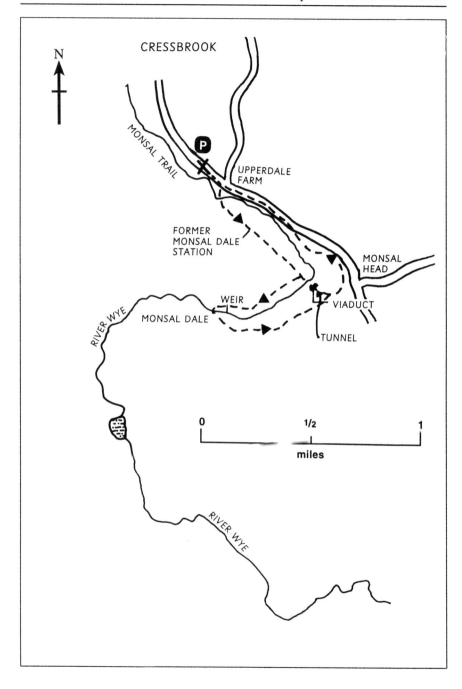

descending, however, it is interesting to walk across the viaduct to the mouth of the tunnel, sealed to prevent access.

Return to the route by the riverside, soon reaching a thundering weir. Cross the river by the footbridge beyond the weir and turn left to return along the far bank. An excellent footpath now climbs steadily through the woods to Monsal Head. Hazel is very prominent among the woodland, with evidence of former coppicing.

To return, go through the gap in the wall opposite the teashop, turning right to descend the stepped path. At a junction keep straight on, passing Netherdale Farm at the bottom of the slope before joining the road and continuing to the car park.

Tea shop at Monsal Head

11. Bakewell and The Monsal Trail

Length:	5 miles
Summary:	A section of the Monsal Trail along the railway trackbed is followed by a short roadside link before the return to Bakewell along a very good field and woodland path. There are no long or arduous ascents or difficulties underfoot.
Car Parking:	Public car park at the site of the former Bakewell railway station, reached by following Station Road (B6408) on the east side of the River Wye. Grid reference 222690.
Map:	Ordnance Survey, Outdoor Leisure No. 24, Peak District, White Peak area. 1:25000.

The Tea Shop

Bakewell is quite a centre for tourists and for walkers, offering an abundance of cafes/tea shops. Two have been selected:

a) The Old Original Bakewell Pudding Shop, The Square. Right in the town centre, this popular restaurant is above the shop. There is a very wide choice of food here, ranging from full cooked meals, including high teas, to tea and cakes. Not to be missed, of course, is Bakewell Pudding. This is the real thing, **the** "pudding" made to a secret recipe, not the universally available "tart" of dubious authenticity.

The surroundings are pleasant and walkers are welcomed. Opening hours are from 9am to 6pm (November to April) and 9am to 9pm (May to October), every day except Christmas Day. Tel. 01629 812193.

b) Harleys – tucked away in a courtyard named Prospect Place. From the main square turn right at the National Westminster Bank, walk 40 yards along Water Street, and turn left into an alleyway leading directly into Prospect Place. On a sunny day, Harleys is at its best as there are outside tables in the attractive sheltered courtyard. Inside, the flagged floor ensures that boots are no problem! Scones, cakes, and the usual range of beverages are available. Open from 10am to 5pm every day except Christmas Day. Tel. 01629 815489.

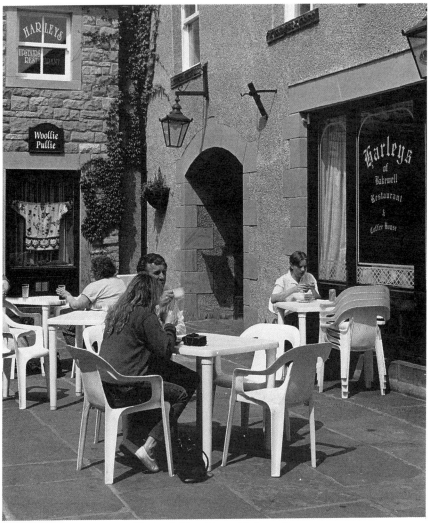

Harley's Tea Shop, Bakewell

Description

Sitting astride the River Wye, the old town of Bakewell is the largest settlement within the Peak District National Park. Granted its charter as long ago as 1330, the town has long been an important centre and the present day comprehensive Monday market is a major attraction both for residents and for visitors.

At one time Bakewell seemed destined to compete with Buxton and Matlock as a spa town, but the potential was never developed. The early 18th century Market Hall has been converted into a National Park and Tourist Information Centre. The parish church is rightly acclaimed both as a building with Norman features and for the rich variety of its monuments, of which the most important are an 8th century Saxon cross in the churchyard and several shattered carved Saxon tombstones in the porch.

Holme Bridge is a very old packhorse bridge, rebuilt in 1664. Upstream is a weir which originally provided the head of water for the town cornmill. Later, the water power situation became more complex as Arkwright (ref. Cromford walk) built the Lumford cotton spinning mill in 1778, needing a reservoir for its large water power demand and interfering with the supply to the corn mill. Cotton mill extensions in 1852 required the supply of even more water, with another reservoir further upstream and a new channel improving the supply to the corn mill. Several wells are "dressed" each year in accordance with the Peak District custom, an ancient pagan rite giving thanks for the supply of the vital, life-sustaining, water. Well dressing was later adapted as a Christian ceremony, first recorded at Tissington in 1758.

But it is for something of comparative triviality that the name Bakewell has long been a household word, although in describing the local gastronomic speciality, "tart" has been erroneously substituted for "pudding" and the product itself has been slightly changed. Fortunately, the real thing is still made and sold locally and can be recommended without reservation.

The site of the former Hassop railway station seems to be a most unlikely place for a major bookshop, but the Country Book Store is well worth a visit. The range of books on local subjects is particularly impressive.

The Walk

Join the Monsal Trail by the left-hand end of the former station building and turn left. The trackbed rises gently through the pleasant countryside, for some distance on an embankment, soon reaching the bookshop on the site of the former Hassop station. Not surprisingly, this station, sited more than a mile from the small village which it ostensibly served, was closed many years before the line as a whole. With or without a diversion to visit the bookshop, continue along the track, passing high above the A6020 road and then under a farm accommodation bridge.

At the next intersection descend to the right to join a road, turning left under the former railway bridge. Join a more major road (A6020) and turn left to walk alongside the road (there is a footpath). In about 300 yards, opposite Dowcliffe House, turn right at a signpost and stile to take a grassy path heading for a wooded scarp. The path rises steadily through Cracknowl Wood at a reasonable gradient, sections being a little muddy in wet weather.

From the stile at the top of the wood head for the left-hand end of the plantation, where Cracknowl House sits in a hollow. The house is passed through a gate in the wall to the left and the route, not well-marked on the ground, continues up the brow of the next field in more or less the same direction, eventually converging with the wall to the left just over the top of the hill, by a lone tree.

The spire of Bakewell parish church comes into view. Go over a stile just beyond the tree and the path is now more obvious as it bends to the left downhill towards the town. Go through a gate by a dew-pond and continue past a disused quarry, then past a small industrial area before reaching the River Wye at the packhorse bridge. After the river, the corn mill leat is crossed. A portion of this waterway, on the right, was formerly used as a sheep dip.

Turn left to walk alongside the A6 main road to the town centre. The corn mill building is passed in less than 200 yards, the gaunt skeleton of its water wheel still apparent at the rear. The Original Bakewell Pudding Shop and Tea Room is found on the right after passing the Rutland Arms and the Red Lion hotels.

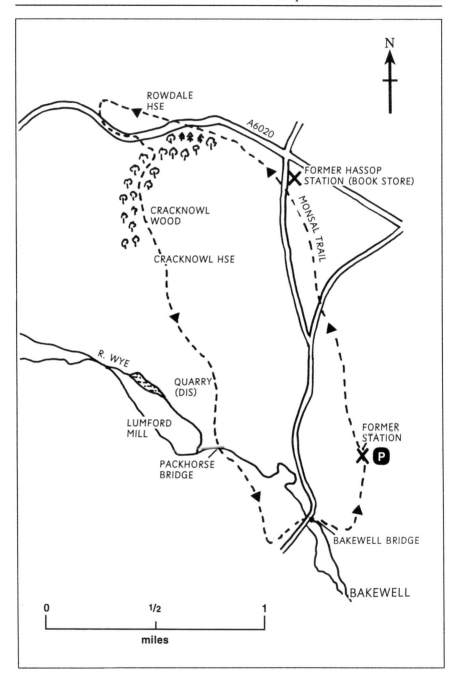

N

ROWDALE
HSE

A6020

FORMER HASSOP
STATION (BOOK STORE)

MONSAL TRAIL

CRACKNOWL
WOOD

CRACKNOWL HSE

R. WYE

QUARRY
(DIS)

LUMFORD
MILL

FORMER
STATION

PACKHORSE
BRIDGE

BAKEWELL BRIDGE

BAKEWELL

0   1/2   1

miles

From the teashop continue in the same direction, cross Bakewell Bridge over the river, and bear right to follow an "industrial estate" sign. Follow Station Road to the car park. At this stage many walkers will probably be having unkind thoughts of the former Duke of Rutland, whose refusal to allow the railway line to follow its natural course through his land at Haddon Hall necessitated both a tunnel and the highly inconvenient siting of Bakewell station such a long trudge from the town centre.

Stone coffins at Bakewell church

12. Calton Lees and Edensor

Length:	4 miles.
Summary:	A first rate ramble through part of the Chatsworth estate, with no serious ascent. Excellent underfoot throughout.
Car Parking:	Large public car park at Calton Lees, by the side of the main Baslow to Matlock road. Grid reference: 259686.
Map:	Ordnance Survey Outdoor Leisure No. 24, Peak District, White Peak area, 1:25000.

The Tea Shop

Entry to the Stables Tea Room at Edensor is through the delightful little shop and post office. Although there is a "no muddy boots" sign, walkers are made very welcome and it is well worth removing dirty footware for the pleasure of visiting this tea shop. White painted stone walls, circular tables with Windsor backed chairs in dark wood, and fitted carpet all contribute to an enjoyable break. Soup, salads, pate and toast, Derbyshire cream teas, full afternoon tea including sandwiches, tea and coffee, are all available in this highly recommended tea shop in a lovely village.

Opening hours are from 10am to 5pm every day except Tuesdays from Easter to the end of October. From November until Easter, 10am to 4pm daily except Tuesdays and Saturdays. Closed for two weeks at Christmas/New Year. Tel. 01246 582283.

Description

The western part of the wide-ranging Chatsworth estate embraces rolling countryside, mostly open, but including New Piece Wood, part of the landscaping originally carried out by Capability Brown. This walk is surprisingly varied, and the return along the side of the

River Derwent is entirely delightful. A diversion to visit any or all of the attractions of Chatsworth House (ref. Walk 13) can, of course, be included.

Edensor (pronounced "Ensor") is an estate village largely housing Chatsworth employees, spaciously laid out around the church on its knoll. The village has, however, a much longer history, being mentioned in the Domesday Book as "Edensoure". At its peak, the cottages reached the River Derwent close to the present bridge. Acquisition of the village by the Cavendish (Devonshire) family was in 1549; it has remained in the same ownership ever since.

In creating the Chatsworth parkland, the 4th Duke demolished that part of the village which was visible from the west front of the House. The 6th Duke continued the demolition, constructing the present village in replacement between 1839 and 1841. Very few buildings of the earlier village remain, one of them being the post office/tea room. The old church was demolished a few years later, the present St. Peter's being consecrated in 1870.

Post Office and Stables tea room, Edensor

The Walk

Start along the tarmac roadway at the south end of the car park, keeping to the right of the entrance to the garden centre. The roadway soon bends to the right, losing its surface after passing the hamlet of Calton Lees.

Go straight on at a farm gate with blue arrow to rise steadily along the bottom of the broad, lush, pheasant-infested, valley for the best part of one mile.

At Calton Houses a sign gives the route of the footpath, up to the right, then looping back through the farm gate with blue arrow, passing the house, and continuing along a stony track between walls.

After passing through a gate, fork right, initially by the side of a wall. At a signposted junction, continue towards "Edensor" to a gate and stile and a walled lane descending through a belt of mainly coniferous woodland. As the woodland is left at a farm gate with high stile, there are marvellous views to Chatsworth House and the Hunting Tower (ref. Walk 13). An information board gives a potted history of the development of the estate.

A route worn across the broad acres of meadow heads for Edensor church, the slender spire standing out ahead. Keep left of a fenced plantation and continue towards the church, bearing left to a gate and steps leading to the public road in the village. Turn right, then bear right around the base of the church mound to reach the post office and tea shop in its little cul de sac.

After refreshments turn right to leave Edensor, cross the main road, and take the wide easy track leading to the road bridge which gives access to the House. Do not cross the bridge (unless, of course, you wish to visit the House and/or gardens), but cross the main drive and follow the path along the side of the river. On reaching the damaged building of the former estate corn mill, turn right towards the road, then left to regain the car park.

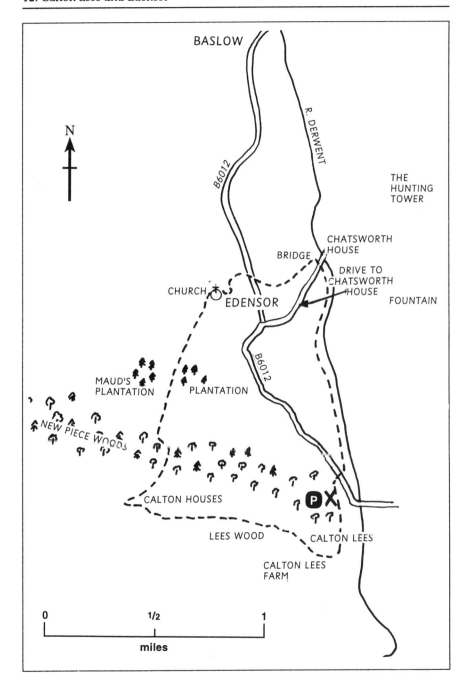

13. Chatsworth

Length:	4½ miles
Summary:	The majority of this walk lies within the parkland surrounding the stately home of Chatsworth. Outside the park there is the rising lane which gives access to Beeley Hill Top, and a footpath climbing to the edge of Beeley Hill Moor. The ascent totals about 500 feet but the gradients are never severe and there are no difficulties underfoot.
Car Parking:	Large free public car park at Calton Lees, by the side of the B6012 road, one mile south of the Chatsworth main entrance. Grid reference: 259686.
Map:	Ordnance Survey, Outdoor Leisure No. 24, Peak District, White Peak area. 1:25000

The Tea Shop

This tea shop is in complete contrast to most of the others recommended in this book. It is large and elegant and, being part and parcel of a famous and popular stately home, the clientele ranges from lone walkers to organised coach parties, including many foreign visitors. A self-service system is operated. The environment is quite spectacular: walls covered with acres of oil paintings, presumably of former members of the Cavendish family, compete for the attention with an old horse drawn coach mounted on a gallery. At the other end of the human spectrum, the fine toilet accommodation has won national awards. Don't be put off by all this magnificence! Walkers are genuinely welcome here and there is a wide range of food and drink to appeal to all tastes available on an all day basis. Cooked meals, salads, soup, scones, cakes, tea, coffee, cold drinks are all included.

Opening hours are from 1st. April (Easter if earlier) to 31st. October, 10am to 5.30pm every day. Te. 01246 582204.

Description

The name Chatsworth has long been a household word for a stately home on the grandest scale. Of Elizabethan origins, the building was much altered between 1686 and 1707, with further large scale additions in the 1820s. Still the home of the Duke and Duchess of Devonshire (Cavendish family), this magnificent house is encircled by 100 acres of almost equally famous gardens, with cascades, fountains, maze, and many other features attracting large numbers of visitors. A farmyard and adventure playground are of particular interest to children. Entry to these various visitor attractions is, of course, subject to opening hours and to payment.

Perhaps a little less well-known is that there are 1000 acres of parkland, with landscaping by Capability Brown, surrounding the house and gardens and that many miles of trackway are open to those on foot, without charge, within this huge and varied area.

Chatsworth House and bridge

A circular walk, as suggested below, can obviously be combined with a visit to the house and/or gardens should this be desired. The all-important tea shop is, of course, accessible to walkers without entering any area requiring payment.

The Walk

From the Calton Lees car park turn right, down the road, to cross the bridge over the River Derwent. At Beeley Lodge take the second roadway on the left, soon commencing the long rise towards Beeley Moor.

After passing the large farmstead at Beeley Hill Top, the lane loses its surface and a stile with a signpost "concessionary footpath to (inter alia) Baslow" is reached. Turn left here and cross a small field diagonally to a stile and gate. A well-marked path rises gently to the left towards the edge of Beeley Moor, with great views over part of the Chatsworth estate and the Derwent valley generally.

Join an unsurfaced farm roadway at the top of the rise and bear left, entering the mature broad leafed woodland of the Chatsworth estate at a gate and stile. Stay with the main track, going straight across towards "Robin Hood" (didn't this man travel!) at a cross-roads. After a right-hand bend, the isolated Park Farm is seen across the fields to the right. After a left-hand bend, keep left at a fork, now descending slightly. Swiss Lake, with Swiss Cottage on the far shore, is now close on the right.

Continue through mixed woodland, with a glimpse of a smaller lake on the right, soon reaching the large Emperor Lake. After bending around the far end of the lake, fork left as the Hunting Tower is approached. This is a tall, narrow building with a sensational site on the edge of the scarp behind and above the main Chatsworth House.

From the tower descend to rejoin the main trackway. There is now a choice of route down to the house. The roadway descends by an easy but, of necessity, circuitous route. The direct route leaves the roadway below the tower and is so steep that it contains a large number of steps, without handrails, including one very long wind-

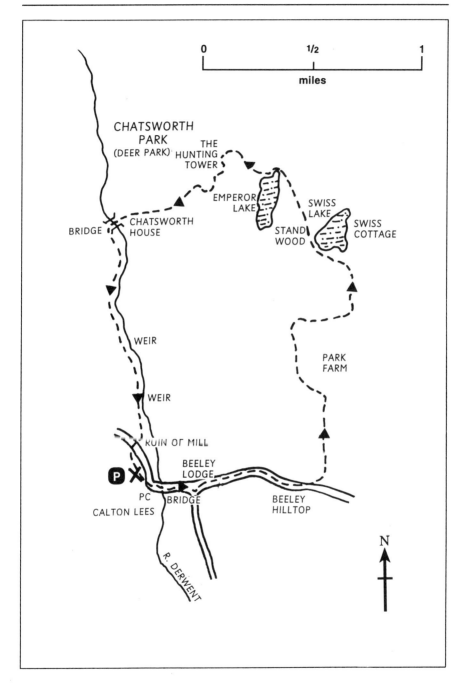

ing flight. A notice warns of the potentially slippery surface of the steps.

Having taken the direct route, turn left at a more major track, near the bottom of the descent, then right in 100 yards or so at a "way out" sign on a stone. Turn right at a surfaced road, passing the farm yard and the adventure playground on the right, and go over a cattle grid, heading for the now obvious main building complex. The restaurant and tea room is in the courtyard of the first building reached.

From the restaurant, go straight across the courtyard to descend past the main house and the house entrance and take a gravel track heading for the road bridge over the river. There are statues on the downstream side of the bridge piers. Cross the bridge and turn sharp left immediately to follow a popular riverside footpath for more than one mile, passing two weirs before reaching the ruin of a mill. Turn right here to ascend to the road by a gate and cattle grid and return to the car park.

14. Over Haddon and Lathkill Dale

Length:	3¾ miles
Summary:	This is very much a walk of two contrasting parts, outward along the bottom of the celebrated Lathkill Dale, with the return along a quiet upland roadway, allowing long and wide views. The descent into Lathkill Dale is by a steep lane, whilst the corresponding rise is on a superb grassy footpath in an apparently unnamed dale. The whole walk is exceptionally good underfoot.
Car Parking:	Pay and display car park, with public conveniences, in Over Haddon. Grid reference, 203665. (About two thirds of the way down the lane into Lathkill Dale, there are spaces for seven or eight cars on the roadside).
Map:	Ordnance Survey, Outdoor Leisure, No. 24, Peak District, White Peak area. 1:25000

The Tea Shop

No problem about boots here – walkers are very welcome although the Courtyard Tea Room does attract many car visitors. It is part of the Lathkill Dale Craft Centre and shares a modern courtyard development with a book binder, a book shop, antique dealer, and other art and craft shops. Inside, original paintings and dried flower arrangements form attractive decoration and are available for sale. Outside are attractive tables and chairs in a sheltered environment.

A good choice of informal meals includes savoury pancakes, filled jacket potatoes, toasted tea cakes, scones, and home-made cakes. There is a vast range of tea, including many of the fruit varieties, plus coffee and cold drinks.

Opening hours are from 10am to 5pm every day, but at weekends only in mid-winter. Tel. 01629 815058.

Former Mandale Mine engine house, Lathkill Dale

Description

Over Haddon village sits high on the rim above the most attractive sections of the acclaimed Lathkill Dale. Formerly part industrial, this valley now includes the Lathkill Dale National Nature Reserve. Still visible are the above ground remains of the Mandale lead mine, mainly a part of the former engine house. Most impressive is the leat which brought water for the wheel from more than ½ mile upstream, first along the far side of the valley, then crossing high over the river on stone piers, still partially surviving.

The Walk

Follow the lane going steeply downhill from the car park, passing the trim but not very old St. Anne's church on the way down to Lathkill Lodge, close to the footbridge over the river. This is a very old water mill site.

Thirty yards before the river turn right at a gate and stile to enter the nature reserve. The flora and fauna are suitably rich along this lovely wooded valley, and the river has a series of weirs and ponds for fish management purposes. In years gone by the valley was also quite an industrial area, as evidenced by the occasional mine entrance tunnel and, a short diversion to the right, the remains of the Mandale lead mine. The track along the dale is good and unmistakeable, reaching a large weir which was the take off point for the Mandale mine.

Leave the nature reserve at a gate and stile and, in a few yards, turn sharp right. As the turn is made, a waterfall can be seen further up Lathkill Dale.

A good, grassy, path now climbs steeply up a pleasant "dry" dale to a gate and stile below a cliff. A walled lane follows another stile and gate and Haddon Grove Farm is passed before the public road is reached.

Turn right for the easy and unremarkable return to Over Haddon. The road really is quiet (8 vehicles on an early April Saturday) and there is generally an adequate verge. The extensive views soon

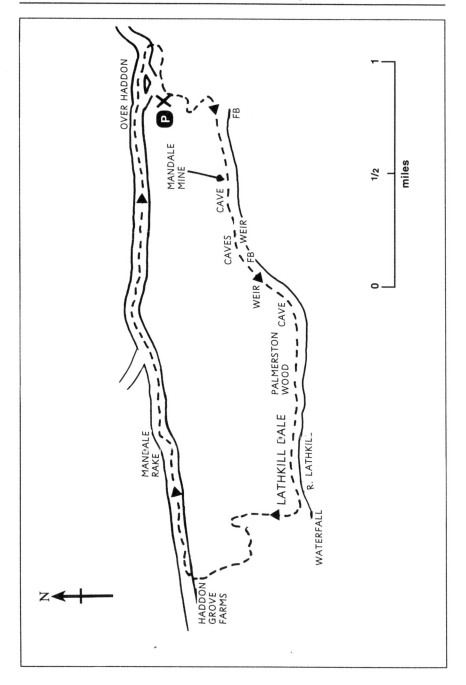

include Over Haddon village. But, can it be real? Or, perish the thought, could it, as it appears in the hazy distance, be some sort of mirage, cruelly deceiving those who, with tongues hanging out plod their weary way across this seemingly interminable plateau in search of the life restoring pot of tea?

Also in view are Stanton Moor, with Stanton in Peak village prominent, and the distant moors beyond the Derwent. Closer at hand the scene is dominated by countless miles of limestone walls, mainly in straight lines but with some twists and turns to follow boundaries which were probably determined in medieval times.

Eventually the Over Haddon boundary sign is reached; never was the entrance to Mecca more joyously acclaimed by the arriving pilgrims. Ignore the road fork leading directly to the car park and continue to the far end of the village, turning right to the tea shop behind the craft centre. From the tea shop turn right and right again to return to the car park.

15. Alport, Youlgreave and Lower Lathkill Dale

Length:	5¼ miles
Summary:	Easy walking almost all the way, with sections of two delightful dales linked by a path across high farmland. Both Alport and Youlgreave have interesting and attractive features. Only the ascent of the side of Lathkill Dale is in any way strenuous.
Car Parking:	Informal parking areas on both sides of the road in Alport. Grid reference: 220646.
Map:	Ordnance Survey, Outdoor Leisure No. 24, Peak District, White Peak area. 1:25000

The Tea Shops

In the first edition of this book, we recommended **Meadow Cottage**, below the village hall of Youlgreave and on the route of this walk. Sadly, this is now only a tea *garden* with drinks served in disposable containers. There is still the usual selection of sandwiches, scones, cakes, tea, coffee, and other beverages. Opening is ocasuual and weekends only in the winter. Tel. 01629 636523.

Fortunately, alternatives are available: if the weather is kind, you should consider a diversion to **Conksbury Farm** (from the route, left uphill for 50 metres from Conksbury Bridge) where Mrs Dale has been serving teas, scones and cakes for over 25 years. The view over Lathkill Dale is delightful – and real crockery is used! Seasonal opening, usually from 10.30 to 5.30pm.

If you prefer a *proper* tea room you need to make a minor diversion to Over Haddon, at the far end of the walk. The ten-minute climb out of the dale (with seats along the way!) takes you to the very top of the hill, with the car park and toilets on your left and the **Yew Tree Tearoom** on your right. This friendly establishment is run by Ian and Adele Gregory, who offer an appealing range of home-baked good-

Yew Tree Tearoom, Over Haddon

ies, including cakes, scones, Bakewell tart and more substantial
meals. From March to the end of October it is open every day, 10.30
to at least 5pm; November to February, weekends only from 11.00 to
5pm – or until the last customer has been served. Tel: 01629 814035.

Description

Alport is a charming hamlet, with bridges, former mill and old cottages, all to be seen only by leaving the main road and walking round
the little back road by the river.

Youlgreave is a much bigger village, stretching at great length
along its principal road. There are houses of the early 17th century
and a parish church with some surviving Norman work, although
the splendidly massive tower dates from the 15th century. The east
window has glass by the eminent pre-Raphaelites, Burne-Jones and
William Morris. Inside the church are a 12th century font, an alabas-
ter tomb, and other interesting features.

A short way along the main street from the church is the conduit
head of 1829, a 1500 gallon tank supplied by a spring at Morstone,
which was the original village public water supply. Opposite, is the
boldly dominant former Co-operative store, now a youth hostel.

Primitive bridge, Lathkill Dale

The Walk

Descend along the road for a short distance. Turn left at a gate and stile, signposted "Conksbury", opposite a public telephone box. A wide, heavily used, track with occasional squeezer stiles follows the bottom of this broad and tranquil part of Lathkill Dale until a lane is reached, close to Raper Lodge. The lane crosses the river by an old packhorse bridge. Go straight across the lane and continue to join a minor public road. If you turn left at this point and go uphill, you will reach Conksbury Farm and its tea garden (see introduction). Otherwise, turn right and cross Conksbury Bridge, another former packhorse bridge. Here, there is a weir and a curious man-made island upstream of the bridge.

After the bridge, turn left at a farm-type gate. The well-made track is now even easier as it hugs the bank of the river. Management of the flow of the water for fishing purposes, over a long period of time, has produced a series of weirs and pools, with notably clear water and plenty of water fowl, the busy coots being much in evidence.

Part of Over Haddon is visible, perched on the rim, as the dale becomes more gorge-like and the woodland thickens on both sides of the river. A little way before reaching the riverside house (formerly a mill site), a "natural" section of river shows how the waterway would probably have looked without large scale human interference.

You now have a choice: either a climb out of the dale to the tea shop, followed by a return to this point, or a continuation of the basic route.

To visit the tea shop at Over Haddon: turn right and walk uphill for up to ten minutes. You pass the car park and toilets on your left and the Yew Tree Tearoom is on your right, with the welcoming "Muddy Boots and All Welcomed". After your visit, walk back downhill (only five minutes this time!) to rejoin the route.

To continue the basic route: if you have not gone to Over Haddon, turn left to cross the footbridge; if you have been to the tea shop, you will see the bridge – of primitive "clapper" construction, with a ford

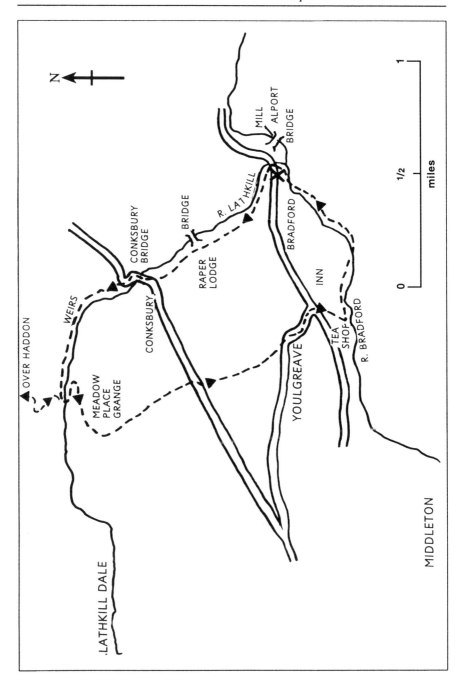

beside – as you return to the dale. Having crossed the river, ascend the far bank on a good stony track through the dense woodland which, perhaps surprisingly, includes rhododendron. From the top of the rise Over Haddon is well seen across the top of the gorge. Turn left beyond the farm gate to follow the line indicated by the signpost towards the large Meadow Place Grange farmstead, of monastic origin as an outlying sheep-farming "grange" of Leicester Abbey.

The route passes through the middle of the farm, with signposts. Leave the farm at a high stile and muddy area by a "Youlgreave" signpost. Angle towards the wall on the left and, as the path rises, look back towards Over Haddon, apparently curiously close, and with the intervening width and depth of Lathkill Dale now totally out of sight. From this high ground, Stanton Moor, with communications mast, stands out well to the south-east. Stay close to the wall, walking easily on good grass and crossing just one stile mid-way until a public road is reached.

Turn right, then left in 40 yards, go over two tight squeezer stiles, and follow a just discernible path with Youlgreave village in view below, beyond a small and sparse plantation. A walled lane is reached, descending steadily to a minor pubic road. Bear left into Youlgreave. At a road fork, go left to the church and village centre, right to continue along the line of the walk.

The route continues practically straight across the main street into Holywell Lane by the telephone box. Descend past the village hall and the public conveniences towards the River Bradford. Meadow Cottage tea garden is near the bottom, on the right.

The last lap follows the very evident "Limestone Way" along the gentle dale, starting either at the stile opposite the tea shop or going to the bottom of the lane and turning left. In half a mile, a minor road is crossed into a broad stony track, bearing left to reach yet another fine packhorse bridge. Don't cross, but keep straight on with the river on the left. Go along a surfaced road for a short distance then take a gate/stile on the left to stay close to the river, passing along the foot of a plantation before joining the road in Alport, a few yards below the car parking areas.

16. Rowsley and Stanton Moor

Length:	6½ miles
Summary:	This is a rewarding but demanding walk, particularly as the prolonged ascent from the valley bottom (nearly 600 feet) to Stanton Moor occurs after the refreshment break. Subject to the odd muddy section, most of the footpaths are very good indeed and there is only the odd place where care in route finding is necessary.
Car Parking:	Informal layby beside the road from Stanton in Peak to Birchover, just up the hill from Stanton. Grid reference: 243638.
Map:	Ordnance Survey Outdoor Leisure No. 24, Peak District, White Peak area. 1:25000.

The Tea Shop

The Country Parlour at Caudwell's Mill is part of a visitor complex which includes both the renovated mill and premises occupied by various craftsmen. Despite its external appearance, the Country Parlour is quite delightful: structural materials are all re-cycled, including beams from Scottish mills, and seating and serving counter salvaged from Crich Carr chapel. As the floor is flagged, walkers' boots cause no problem.

Until noon, light refreshments such as scones and cakes, with tea, coffee and cold drinks are available. From noon onwards, good quality whole-food home cooked meals can also be purchased. Everything is home-made, using flour ground in the adjacent mill.

Opening hours are from 10am to 6pm daily from April to October. 10am to 4.30pm daily during November and December. 10am to 4.30pm Saturday and Sunday only during January and February. Tel. 01629 733185.

Nine Ladies stone circle, Stanton Moor

Description

Stanton Moor is a rather unusual gritstone area isolated within the predominantly limestone countryside of the White Peak, its geology being confirmed by the prevalence of silver birch, rhododendron, and heather vegetation. Stanton Moor Edge is a typically steep gritstone scarp with some interesting tors and other rock features.

Many burial mounds, the odd standing stone and, above all, the Nine Ladies stone circle are evidence of early Bronze Age occupation of the moor. In more modern times man has made substantial inroads by extensive stone quarrying, most of the sites now being disused. Prominent above Stanton Moor Edge is a stone tower erected by Earl Grey (of tea fame?) in 1832 to commemorate the passage of the Parliamentary Reform Bill.

Rowsley can hardly be regarded as one of the Peak District's showpiece villages, particularly bearing in mind its partially industrial past and present and its bisection by the main A6 road. It does, however have a quietly attractive street to the north of the main road and it is the village nearest to the celebrated Haddon Hall. Caudwell Mill and Working Craft Centre is a complex which includes a restored corn mill and several separately operated craft workshops open to visitors throughout the year, although the mill itself has more limited times of operation.

The Walk

Walk down to Stanton village and turn right at the first road junction to take a minor road signposted "Stanton Lees". As the road levels out above woodland, turn right at a stile signposted "footpath via stone circle". A broad, well-used, path heads for the edge of a wood and then continues just inside the wood. Keep to what is obviously the main track until the stone circle is reached, just 50 yards to the right.

From the stone circle return to the main track and cross over to follow a lesser path heading directly for the "Reform" Tower, soon visible through the trees. From the top of the scarp a great deal of the broad valley of the River Derwent, partially industrialised, is visible.

Go over the stile by the tower and turn right along a good path keeping close to the scarp edge. The way is easy to follow and the gritstone features, which add interest along the way, include a rock inscribed EIN 1831, the earliest and by far the best executed act of vandalism on this particular stone. The views over the valley are extensive. The path bears right as a steady descent begins, making for a minor road, with Barn Farm in view ahead.

However, more than 100 yards short of the road, immediately after passing a prominent (and final) tor, look carefully for a narrow but distinct path curving to the left, round the back of the tor. This lightly-used path could easily be missed. It is the start of an old trackway, well-constructed as a terrace along the face of the scarp, apparently for long defunct quarry purposes. The path is a little overgrown but is easy to follow as it takes a generally descending

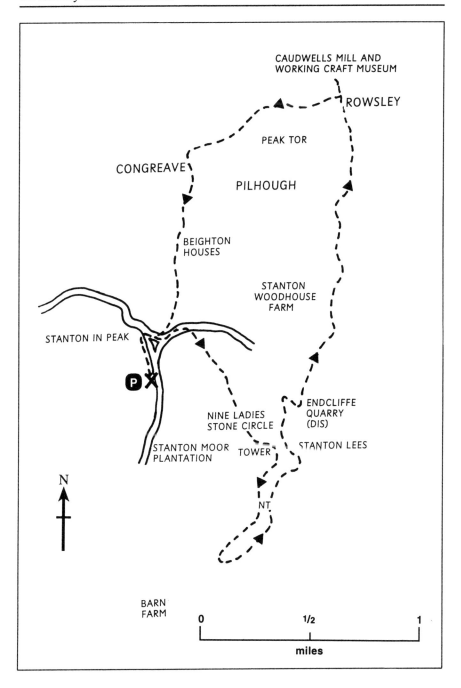

line for more than one mile, passing above the hamlet of Stanton Lees, to a large disused quarry with starkly ruinous buildings.

The quarry access roadway leads to a minor public road. Turn right for 100 yards or so and then left over a rudimentary stile by a farm gate. Follow an obvious path across the field, soon bearing left along the rim of another disused quarry, with the substantial farmstead of Stanton Woodhouse ahead. Northwood village, sprawling up the far valley side is prominent as Stanton Woodhouse, with some very old farm buildings, is reached.

Beyond the farm, as the roadway zig zags, there is a signposted short-cutting footpath, then the farm roadway provides the rest of the route to join the public road at Rowsley, just short of the bridge over the River Wye. The huge corn mill, craft centre and tea shop, with its prominent roof ventilators, is accessed through its car park, on the left.

The return route re-crosses the river, turning right along the road towards Pilhough and Stanton in Peak, past the recreation and cricket grounds. As the road bends left, uphill, go straight ahead at a gate and stile to follow a signposted path rising across the meadow, well below the little wooded knobble of Peak Tor. As the path becomes less obvious, aim for the right-hand end of a small plantation, where there is a stile, a tiny stream and a second stile, followed by a just visible path on the grassy shoulder ahead. The hamlet of Congreave is entered at a stile. Turn left at the surfaced road and ascend steeply. Just above the hamlet turn right at an unsignposted farm gate to take a footpath close to the wall on the left. Several stiles confirm the route, which rises, steeply at the end, to join a road at a stile.

Turn right, pass a stone-built belvedere and then Beighton Houses, and turn left to take a signposted path rising into the woodland. The gradient soon eases after a wall is passed. The path emerges from the woodland by the side of Stanton cricket ground. Carry on to the public road and bear right, downhill, to the junction. Turn left to return to the car park.

17. Elton and Harthill Moor

Length:	4¼ miles
Summary:	A good little tramp across Harthill Moor, with a fair amount of rise and fall, and with fine landscape features and historical interest.
Car Parking:	Roadside parking along the side of the main street in Elton, reasonably near to the church. Grid reference: 222609.
Map:	Ordnance Survey, Outdoor Leisure No. 24, Peak District, White Peak area, 1:25000.

The Tea Shop

To reach the combined guest house/cafe in Elton, turn up Moor Lane, opposite the church. On a sunny day, the outside tables will appeal; inside, the decoration includes a large collection of old advertising signs.

The range of food on offer includes some cooked meals – the chips looked delicious – and the usual tea, coffee, other beverages, and cakes. Indicated opening days are Saturdays, Sundays, and Bank Holiday Mondays in the summer months and Sundays only during the winter. More than most, a quick phone call to confirm is suggested in this case. Tel 01629 650217.

Description

Elton is by no means one of the Peak District's showpiece villages, but its sturdy sense of purpose, with farmhouses still evident on the main street, compensates for any lack of superficial prettiness.

Like nearby Stanton Moor, Harthill Moor is one of the district's most important areas of early occupation, with surviving relics of the Bronze and Iron ages and the ancient trading route known as the

Tea shop, Elton

Portway. More recent is the "Hermit's Cave", where the carving of a crucifix in the living rock is believed to be of the 12th century and may or may not have been the work of a resident hermit. Coupling the historic with the fine geological and scenic features, such as the gritstone masses of Robin Hood's Stride and Cratcliffe, within its small area the moor offers a great deal of interest for the visitor.

The Walk

Start along Well Street, beside the church, soon forking left at a signpost "public footpath Youlgreave". At a farm gate with narrow stile (yellow arrow on post), fork left and then angle half right, turning sharp right at a signpost in 20 yards. Keep close to the hedge as the meadow is descended to the squeezer stile in the bottom right-hand corner. A pleasant grassy track is always obvious ahead as it rises to a minor road. Prominent to the left is Anthony Hill, with its steep scarp on one side.

Cross the road, negotiate more squeezers, bear right, then left, to follow a just visible path on grass to a wooden stile. Continue, now on more or less level ground, with long views to the high ground above Haddon Hall on the far side of the Wye valley and, further right, the high moors to the east of the Derwent valley.

The access trackway to Cliff Farm is crossed, the stile on the far side being about 40 yards beyond the track. As the way heads for Tomlinson Wood, Alport village is seen, ahead and below. At the last stile before the wood, bend a little left towards a finger post on the far side of the field and then follow the edge of the wood. At a signpost "Robin Hood's Stride" go straight on.

Harthill Moor Farm is on the top of the rise ahead, but the ill-defined path aims a little to the left of the line of telegraph poles, to a stile in a wall. Fifty yards after the stile turn right to climb a muddy track leading to the farm. From the top of the rise, Youlgreave is the village prominent to the north-west. Behind the farm and not readily seen is an iron age hill fort.

Follow the obvious route round the farm buildings, then turn right into a lane leading to a public road. Go over the stile on the opposite

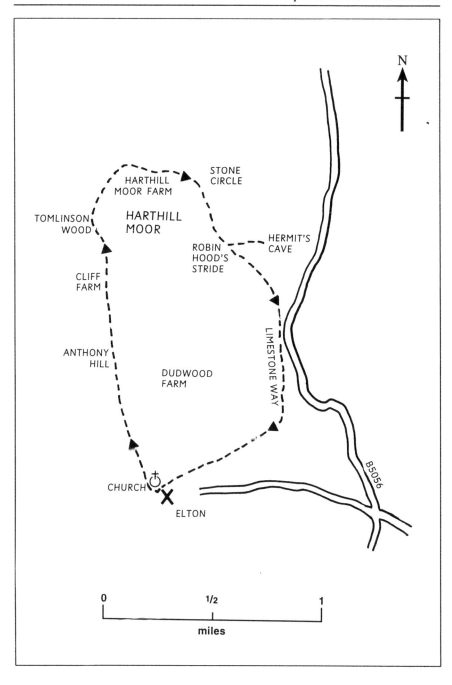

side of the road to follow a signposted path aiming towards the left-hand side of the impressive rocky outcrop ahead. Seen against the sunlight, it is not difficult to appreciate how this outcrop came by its alternative name of "Mock Beggar Hall"

Well before reaching the rocks, look to the left; in the next field are the four large standing stones which are all that remains of an original bronze age circle of nine. Unfortunately, there is no public right of way to the stones. Robin Hood's Stride is the official name for the rock outcrop, the legend being that the famous outlaw could stride from one pinnacle to the other. Nearby, the rocks of the top of Cratcliffe form another impressive landscape feature.

Cratcliff Tor

From an exploration of Robin Hood's Stride, descend to cross the main path, stay close to the top of the woodland, go to the right, over a broken wall, then a stile, to reach the hermit's cave in a further 50 yards. Return by the same route or, alternatively, cut a corner by angling down through the woodland to reach a stile at the bottom edge, rejoining the main path lower down. This main path is now the designated "Limestone Way", but its origins as part of the Portway are lost in antiquity, pre-dating the Roman occupation.

Join the Cratcliffe Cottage access roadway and descend to the public road, reached at a stile. Bear right to take the minor road, climbing steadily. Just before the crest of the hill turn right at a wooden stile, signposted "Elton". Angle left across the meadow towards neglected and outgrown hawthorn hedging, after which the path is better defined. Bear left across another rising meadow, pass a tennis court, and go left to a stile and farm gate to return to the main street in Elton. Turn right to the church.

18. Cromford and The High Peak Trail

Length: 5 miles.

Summary: Canal towpath, former railway line, field path, and surfaced roadways combine to give a very good, well-varied, circuit, with no difficulty underfoot and only the ascent of the inclined plane requiring any real effort.

Car Parking: At Arkwright's Mill or the pay and display car park across the road. Grid reference: 299570.

Map: Ordnance Survey Outdoor Leisure No. 24, Peak District, White Peak area, 1:25000.

The Tea Shop

This cafe is part of the Arkwright's Mill complex. Whilst the interior is rather plain, it is in character with the surroundings. There is plenty of outdoor seating in the former mill yard. Sitting quietly, with a little imagination one can still hear the clatter of clogs on the cobbles, echoing round the yard, as the workers rushed to clock in at 6am on a dark and dismal winter morning. In addition to tea, coffee, and cold drinks, a range of light snacks, including salads, is available throughout the day. The service is friendly and helpful.

Open 9 – 5pm every day throughout the year except Christmas Day. Tel. 01629 825776.

Description

Cromford is an unassuming little town situated close to the River Derwent, one mile south of Matlock Bath. However, in terms of early industry its place in history is secure. Arkwright's Mill was the first successful water powered cotton mill, extended from time to time to form an impressive complex. It is being progressively restored as a major visitor attraction, incorporating some shops.

Arkwright's Mill

In 1793 the Cromford Canal was opened, serving this mill and other nearby industries, with a connection via the Erewash Canal to the River Trent. In 1830, possibly the best known of all the "canal" railways was partially opened. This was the Cromford and High Peak Railway, providing a link between the Peak Forest Canal at Whaley Bridge and the Cromford Canal at Cromford. This remarkable line weaved its way across the high southern plateau of Derbyshire, necessitating several very substantial rope-hauled inclines, primarily at or close to the two ends of the line, together with what became Britain's steepest locomotive-powered adhesion railway at Hopton incline (gradient 1 in 16). Over the years there were changes, the most important being connections to other railways at either end, and route variations to avoid the inclines on the northern portion. In 1853, the Cromford end was connected at High Peak Junction to the line which became the Midland Railway main line, following which the importance of the canal declined steadily. Locomotive haulage replaced the original horse power at an early date, but the fixed engines remained on the inclines at the Cromford end throughout the life of the line.

The operation of these inclines was not without excitement, most notably in 1888, when a loaded wagon and brake van broke away from the haulage rope, then descending at such a pace that they left the rails at the bottom curve, leapt over the canal and the adjacent Midland Railway main line, ending up in the field which is now the sewage works. Remarkably, sections of this most unlikely of railway lines remained operational until the late 1960s, with a diesel replacing the steam locomotive housed at Sheep Pasture Top. The section included in this walk is part of the designated High Peak Trail; at Middleton Top, just a mile or so further along the Trail, the steam engine has been restored as part of a visitor centre.

Black Rocks is a local beauty spot, easily reached by a short diversion from the visitor centre of the same name.

The Walk

From the car park beyond the mill (or the pay and display car park on the opposite side of the road), start along the towpath of the Cromford Canal, passing the attractive wharves at the canal terminus. Proceed to High Peak Junction, in approximately 1¼ miles. The canal surroundings are pleasantly wooded although quite close to the hustle and bustle of the main A6 road; with canal, railway, and road, there are three adjacent generations of transport history.

The canal is left at High Peak Junction, but a small diversion is highly recommended. Stay on the towpath side of the canal for another ⅓ mile, passing the fine structure of Leawood pumping station with its hexagonal stone chimney, and cross the Leawood aqueduct, which carries the canal over the River Derwent. Note the truncated former branch canal in front of a tumbledown cottage. Having crossed the river 150 yards upstream, the railway disappears into a tunnel close by.

Cross the canal by the swing bridge, similar to that at High Peak Junction, and return to the junction along the other side of the aqueduct, the path passing an interesting building where goods were

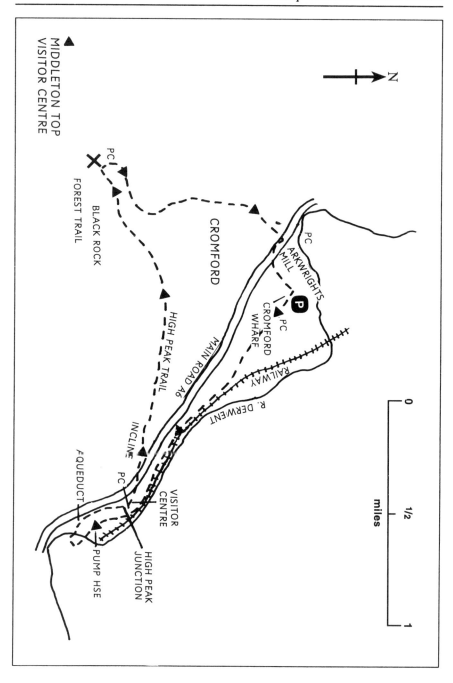

trans-shipped from boats to railway wagons and vice versa. From the junction, which is complete with information centre, old railway workshops, picnic tables, and public conveniences, the path ascends the immense former inclined plane of the Cromford and High Peak Railway. Originally there were two inclined planes, the Cromford (at a gradient of 1 in 9), and the Sheep Pasture (at 1 in 8), with an end to end junction, but in 1857 they were combined and the Cromford engine house became redundant. The combined length is 1291 yards, with a short level section at the former junction; the rise is 400 feet.

Go through the tunnel under the A6 road and rise steadily; the lower part of the incline has views over the Derwent valley. About two thirds of the way up, by a seat on the left, is a small disused quarry, with the remains of a crane. The shell of Sheep Pasture engine house marks the top of the incline, and the seats here encourage leisurely admiration of the extensive views, unfortunately including examples of present day Peak District industry.

Continue along the level portion of the old railway line for a long ½ mile to the Black Rocks visitor centre and picnic area. Now, for the first time, some careful route finding is required. From the visitor centre, back track for 100 yards to a point where there is a farm type gate and a finger post on the left of the old railway line. Take the footpath descending by rudimentary steps on the left side of a wall. Continue downhill through woodland, bending right at a little clearing, along a well-defined path.

On reaching an area of disturbed stony ground, bear right to the far corner, descend a few steps, and take the path along the top edge of a field, soon reaching an unsurfaced roadway via two gates. Carry on down towards Cromford village, close below. Thirty yards after the lane bends left at Holly Cottage, turn right at a tiny footpath, among the outlying houses of the village. Continue into Bedehouse Lane, eventually joining the busy B5036 road just above the village shopping area and with less than ¼ mile to go to the A6 road, which is crossed to reach the minor road and Arkwright's Mill, opposite.

19. Tissington and The Tissington Trail

Length:	4½ miles.
Summary:	The outward section using the Tissington Trail, the trackbed of the former railway line, is entirely gentle, followed by a steady ascent to Bassett Wood Farm for refreshments and an easy return to Tissington.
Car Parking:	Public car park at the site of the former Tissington railway station. Grid reference: 178521.
Map:	Ordnance Survey Outdoor Leisure No. 24, Peak District, White Peak area, 1:25000

The Tea Shop

Do visit Bassett Wood Farm – the Carrington family recently took over the farm, which is part of the important Tissington Estate. You are assured of a warm welcome in this typical farmhouse and will be able to have a pleasant conversation with at least one member of the family. Mrs. Carrington serves a full range of beverages, sand-wiches, home-made cakes and scones, toasted sandwiches, toasted tea-cakes, and ices.

Open every afternoon (may not be open on Wednesdays) and also worth trying at other times. Being a working farm, the hours are somewhat flexible and providing she is at home Mrs. Carrington is willing to provide refreshments.

Farmhouse bed and breakfast is available and there is a small caravan site on the farm. Tel. 01335 350254.

Description

Tissington must come close to everyone's idea of a perfect Peak District village: attractive stone-built houses, with a pond and a spacious green in front of an impressive Elizabethan manor house.

Above all, Tissington claims to have originated the "well-dressing" ceremonies which are such an established part of village life throughout much of Derbyshire. There are several wells in Tissington and the dressing consists of the painstaking construction of religious tableaux using thousands of flowers as the principal material. The dressing is accompanied by a religious service on Ascension Day, processing to the wells in turn, with hymns, psalms and blessings by the Vicar. Although the ceremony is now entirely Christian following its revival in 1758, the origins were long before that date, giving thanks to pagan gods for constant supplies of life-giving water

The parish church opposite the Hall is well worth a visit, the fine chancel arch being just one of many Norman features. One end of the arch is partially obscured by an unusual monument to members of the Fitzherbert family, occupiers of the Hall for more than four centuries. The north aisle is 19th century, but constructed in the Norman style.

Tissington Hall

The Tissington Trail was opened a few years after the closure of the Hartington to Ashbourne section of the Buxton to Ashbourne railway line in 1963 (Buxton to Hartington closed in 1967) This London and North Western line came late in the railway age, being opened in 1899. The line was never really successful in attracting through traffic and the single track was not subsequently doubled, as had been intended and provided for. Locally generated freight and a few passengers from this sparsely populated area were not nearly enough to keep the line open in the competitive situation in the 1960s. The former station at Tissington is now a sizeable car park with information, picnic tables, refreshment stall, and public conveniences.

The Trail is open to walkers, cyclists, and horse riders.

The Walk

Leave the car park at the far end and head south along the trackbed of the former railway, now the Tisssington Trail. Pleasant farming country on the right is complimented by broad leafed woodland on the left and, in about ½ mile, Bassett Wood Farm, site of the recommended teashop, is visible on its hilltop across the valley to the left. Before those with a thirst become too excited, however, it must be said that most walkers will need the best part of an hour before they arrive at the farm and that by this time refreshment will be much more deserved!

After passing over the main Buxton-Ashbourne road, and under a bridge, Fenny Bentley cutting is entered. This is a nature reserve managed by Derbyshire Wildlife Trust. The site of the former Thorpe station, with substantial car park, is soon reached.

Continue for a further 200 yards and turn left to leave the Trail at a point where posts indicate paths to right and left, (for "Fenny Bentley"). Descend a rough grassy field to cross the stream in the bottom on a narrow concrete bridge, and climb the slope opposite to a stile in the fence at the top. The path, always visible on the ground, continues in a straight line, descending towards Fenny Bentley. On reaching a lane at the edge of the village, turn left towards the church and go through the churchyard to the main road.

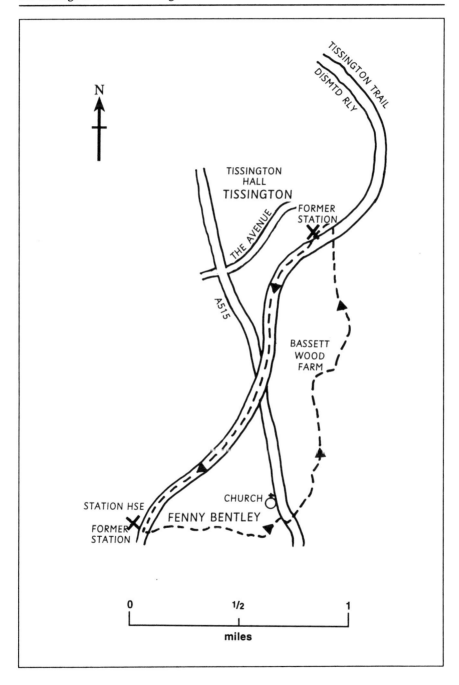

Turn right for a few yards, cross over and, just past the former schoolroom and telephone box, turn left at a signpost "Tissington 2". In 40 yards fork right to cross the stream and rise past a few houses. After the last house on the left, turn left up the meadow, aiming for the angle in the boundary hedge, then stay close to the hedge to the top of the field, where there is a stile with arrow. Over the stile, bend left and follow the hedge across two more large fields, the roofs of the farm complex coming into view ahead. Across the last large field before the farm, aim fractionally to the right of the furthest telegraph pole, reaching the farm approach road over two more stiles. Turn left to the front of the farmhouse for the teashop.

Leave the farm by its access roadway. In about 300 yards turn left to a stile and keep close to the hedge on the left to cross a large field. The line across the next field is diagonal, aiming for the far right corner, through a farm gate, and angling to the public road at the edge of Tissington village. Cross the bridge over the former railway line and turn left to return to the car park.

20. Ilam

Length:	3 miles.
Summary:	A very easy and highly recommended walk, largely in the grounds of Ilam Park, with no lack of interesting features along the way.
Car Parking:	Large car parks (charge made) at foot of Dovedale, close to Ilam and Thorpe Cloud. Grid reference: 146509.
Map:	Ordnance Survey Outdoor Leisure No. 24 The Peak District, White Peak area, 1:25000.

The Tea Shop

This National Trust enterprise is situated in the former stable block at the rear of Ilam Hall. The room itself is large with plain wood furniture and green gingham curtains. Blackboards display the good range of food, available during the whole day. Light lunches, afternoon teas and casual drinks of all kinds are included. Opening hours are from 11am to 5.30pm each day but closed every Wednesday and Thursday (ond of May to end of September) and 11am to 4pm Saturdays and Sundays only during the winter. The teashop closes during the Christmas and New Year period. Tel. 01335 350 245.

Description

Originally owned by the Benedictine Abbey of Burton on Trent, the Ilam Estate was sold to John Port following the dissolution of the monasteries by Henry VIII. The estate remained with this family until it was sold to David Pike-Watts in 1809. On his death it passed to his daughter Mary whose husband, Jesse Watts-Russell, had the house rebuilt on a grand scale, in the Gothic style, between 1821 and 1826. The architect was James Trubshawe.

Ilam Hall, with the garden and church

The present stable-block, now housing the teashop, is believed to be the only surviving part of the earlier house.

As with the house, the gardens were greatly developed at that time, the present Italian Gardens being merely the upper part of a huge area which led down to the River Manifold in terraces. The "Pepper Pot" tower, close to the house entrance, was built by Trubshawe as a dovecote.

Originally of the 12th century, the Church of the Holy Cross was restored in 1618, then enlarged in the time of Jesse Watts-Russell by the addition of the octagonal mausoleum, housing the marble monument to David Pike-Watts. The font is the oldest surviving feature, claimed to be Saxon, with carvings depicting scenes from the life of St. Bertram. In the churchyard are two Saxon crosses.

The legend claims that St. Bertram spent the latter years of his life as a hermit in a small grotto in the bank of the River Manifold, taking drinking water from the nearby well, now within a walled enclosure. On the hillside above this grotto is another shallow cave equipped with stone table and bench. Here, as a youth of nineteen, William

Ilam: the "pepper pot"

Congreve (1670-1729) is believed to have written one of his stage comedies.

At the road junction outside the grounds of the Hall is a striking monument to the wife of Jesse Watts-Russell.

In the late 1920s most of the Hall was demolished. The remaining portion was bought by Sir Robert McDougall and presented to the National Trust for use as a youth hostel. The Trust owns and manages the Park, with shop, information centre and tea room.

The Walk

Cross the road by the entrance to the main part of the car park and head for steps and a track leading to a double stile. Follow the well-marked footpath rising a little to pass behind the extensive Isaak Walton Hotel. In less than one mile, the path joins the Ilam road. Bear right to the large monument at the road junction, then right again, uphill. In 50 yards, opposite the village school, turn left to a gate and stile with a footpath sign. Follow a broad cart track, initially along the edge of a large field. The landscape is typical of a stately home parkland but, a little further, there is surviving evidence of medieval "ridge and furrow" cultivation, perhaps reminding us of the monastic origins of this estate. As the track bends sharply left, go straight on across the lush grass, with scant evidence of a path on the ground for some distance. Aim between a fenced former dew-pond on the left and a rocky hummock on the right.

The route bends a little left before descending a steep, muddy, bank to the side of the River Manifold, close to a footbridge. Turn sharp left to a gate and stile to follow a level footpath known as the "Paradise Walk". The Manifold here has only a little sluggish water, the great majority of the flow having gone underground seven miles or so upstream near Wettonmill (ref. Walk 21).

The path is fringed by superb mature lime and yew trees, and the "battlestone", commemorating a conflict between Danes and Saxons is soon reached. Across the river the fine trees of Hinkley Wood, including many specimens of both large and small leaved limes, cling to the steep hillside.

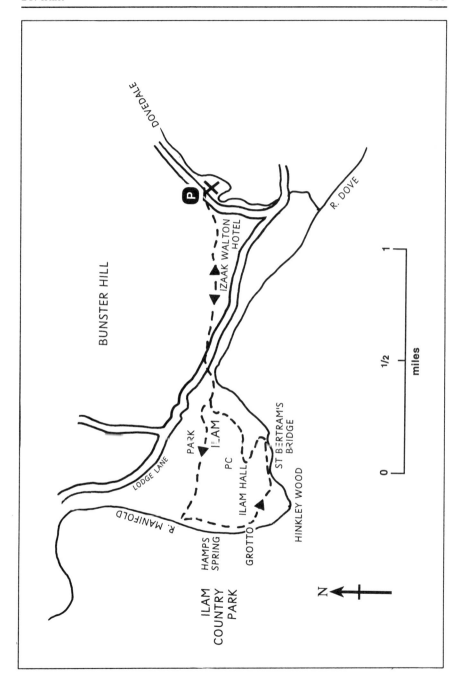

A little further is St. Bertram's grotto; above, reached by flights of steps, is the grotto with stone bench and table, allegedly used by Congreve.

Hereabouts the river becomes much more swollen as large volumes of underground water of the River Manifold and the River Hamps force their way back into main stream at the "boil holes". Go straight ahead to St. Bertram's Bridge, nicely inscribed with its name and "restored 1839". From the bridge return towards the Hall. On the right, enclosed by stone walls, is the clear flowing water in the "well" said to have been used by St. Bertram. To the left is the circular base of a former bandstand.

The tea room is in the former stable block, reached by ascending the steps, crossing the formal garden, and turning left then right to the first floor entrance.

After refreshment, go straight to the church, follow the path to the village, then return to the Dovedale car park along the outward footpath. In this direction the fine profile of Thorpe Cloud is all dominant.

21. Grindon and The Manifold Trail.

Length:	4¾ miles
Summary:	This walk includes the fine section of the Manifold valley between Weag's Bridge and Wettonmill, with a return to Grindon by climbing the flank of Ossom's Hill. The great majority of the route is on good paths, including the metalled trackbed of the former Leek and Manifold Valley railway line.
Car Parking:	Small car park close to Grindon church. Grid reference: 085545.
Map:	Ordnance Survey Outdoor Leisure No. 24 Peak District, White Peak area, 1:25000.

The Tea Shop

Being completely honest this walk is without a tea shop but has been included as we feel that most ramblers in the Peak District would wish to walk at least part of the delightful Manifold Trail.

The cafe at Wettonmill will provide you with refreshments – tea, coffee, crisps, wrapped biscuits. chocolate. etc.

In good weather it is pleasant sitting outside over-looking the river for a few minutes before continuing the walk.

Description

After the Dove, the Manifold has claims to be the most popular valley in the Peak District, with limestone crags, caves and other features in profusion. Indeed, Thor's Cave is of great significance, having provided shelter for bands of "cavemen", hunter/gatherers of the stone age. Unfortunately, the excavation in Victorian times was enthusiastic rather than scientific and much of what was found was not properly recorded. There is a smaller, more accessible, cave at Wettonmill which was similarly used by hunter/gatherers.

The Manifold is an extreme case of the Peak District phenomenon of disappearing water, the river bed becoming dry just below Wettonmill, with no major resurgence until the grounds of Ilam Hall, several miles downstream.

Access to the valley is much facilitated by the use of the trackbed of the former Leek and Manifold Valley Light Railway. Built to the unusual gauge of 2' 6", this optimistic line connecting the North Staffordshire Railway at Waterhouses with the small village of Hulme End was opened in 1904, "starting nowhere and finishing at the same place" in the words of a navvy of the time. The valley was (and is) very little populated, the villages ostensibly served by the line being situated high above the steep valley sides. In the 1930s the tourist trade declined, the creamery at Ecton, a major user of the railway, closed and, in 1934 the line expired. Throughout its comparatively short life, two locomotives and a handful of rolling stock

Bridge at Wettonmill

had sufficed for the light traffic. Although built in Leeds, both locomotives and coaches were of an attractive Indian design.

Wettonmill is an old mill site at a point where a minor road climbs laboriously into and out of the dale.

Grindon village is pleasant enough, sitting high above the valley. Outside the church wall is the very old "Rindle Stone", recording the Lord of the Manor's right to the water of a stream which flows only in the winter.

The Walk

From the car park bear left downhill towards the main part of the village. Note the plaque outside the church: the "Rindle Stone" can be found near the church gates. As the road divides, fork right, turn right again at the more important road, then left in 40 yards at a sign "AA route 132 – Manifold Valley".

In a further 50 yards turn left again to follow a grassy lane towards Buckfurlong Farm. Before reaching the farm buildings, go right, over a stile with public footpath sign. Pass behind the farm buildings, with two more stiles in quick succession. Descend the meadow to a stile with post and continue the same line along the bottom of the broad, shallow, valley. After passing a redundant dew pond, turn left at a gate with blue arrow, keeping close to the wall on the right to rise to a similar gate and the public road. The sinuously curving course of the Manifold Valley in all its beauty is revealed below.

Turn right. There is a footpath cutting off the corner of the road, but the distance saved is scarcely worth the effort of climbing over the stile at each end! From the road turn right at a signposted stile to follow a not very distinct footpath descending steeply to Weag's Bridge. Start by keeping close to the fence on the right.

At the bridge, which spans the usually dry bed of the River Manifold, turn left along the surfaced trackbed of the former light railway, rising very gently along this most attractive valley. The towering limestone rampart on the right, which soon engages the attention, has a surprise on its far side as the gaping hole of Thor's Cave appears, high up the far valley side. A diversion to the famous

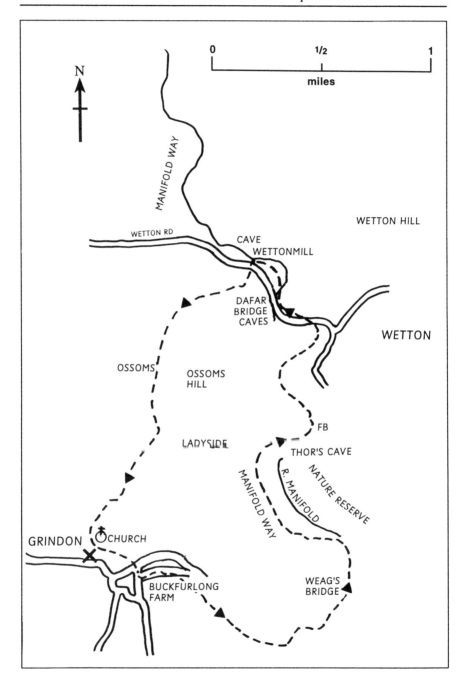

attraction and view point is short but certainly steep. The river bed is crossed by a footbridge.

Back on course, continue along the trackbed. As a public road is reached, take either fork to head for the former corn mill at Wettonmill, now providing refreshments and public conveniences. At the point where the two roads have side by side bridges, the presence of water in the river bed will be noted for the first time. However, this usually disappears just a few yards downstream of the stone bridge. Turn right to enter the Wettonmill complex. On the hillside above Wettonmill and not difficult to reach is the cave used as a shelter by Neolithic hunter/gatherers.

From Wettonmill, re-cross the river, cross a footbridge over a stream, and take the footpath by the National Trust "Ossom's Hill" sign. The path rises steeply to a yellow-capped post. Turn right to a stile and follow a path through fields and over stiles with the top of Ossom's Hill always a little way above to the left. Ossom's Hill Farm is passed and the farm approach road is reached over a final stile. Proceed along this road to return to Grindon church, very obvious on the hill ahead.

22. Dovedale and Alstonefield

Length:	5 miles.
Summary:	Including part of the lovely Dovedale, quiet Hall Dale, the hamlet of Milldale, and the beautifully kept village of Alstonefield, this is a fine, varied, walk with ample reward for the moderate amount of rise and fall involved. Paths are good throughout, with just the steep descent on grass into Milldale requiring extra care.
Car Parking:	Public car park by roadside close to Milldale village. Grid reference: 138548.
Map:	Ordnance Survey Outdoor Leisure No. 24, Peak District, White Peak area, 1:25000.

The Tea Shop

The very typically English Old Post Office Tea Room in Alstonefield is a delightful tea shop in a delightful village. The decor is Olde English, with plain wood tables and chairs – even the place mats are attractive and depict local scenes. Deliberately unmatched bone china cups, saucers and plates add to the charm. A good range of food is available – we sampled coffee – a pot for one costing only what is sometimes charged for a cup produced three cups. homemade cakes and Bakewell slices are highly recommended. Light lunches and set afternoon teas are also available.

During the afternoon at peak periods, it may be that only set teas will be available indoors (when weather permits, the tables in the garden across the road are available). However, the set teas do offer good value for good food in superb surroundings. Walkers are most welcome but are, understandably, asked to remove boots in the hall; overslippers are provided.

Opening hours are from 10.30am to 5pm from March to November, daily except Wednesdays and Thursdays. (closing on Wednesday only in July and August). Tel. 01335 27201

Olde Post Office Cafe, Alstonefield

Description

The upper part of Dovedale, with well-used and well-made footpath, has many natural features of interest, Raven's Tor and Dove Holes being the best known. At Milldale hamlet the ancient packhorse bridge is known as Viator Bridge from an imaginary conversation recorded in Isaak Walton's famous book "The Compleat Angler".

Hall Dale is altogether quieter and less spectacular but is well-known as a rich source of fossils.

Alstonefield, apart from having the recommended tea shop, is a very attractive village on high ground, with a green perfectly placed in front of the inn.

Alstonefield: the village green with the George and Dragon Inn

The Walk

Walk down the road into Milldale village, beautifully situated at a junction of dales. There is a National Trust information barn and outdoor refreshments at Polly's. Upstream, the valley of the River Dove is called Mill Dale, then Wolfscote Dale, then Beresford Dale. As in the case of the River Wye, there is a bewildering choice of name for the valley of one river of modest length. However, downstream there is no problem; the valley of the River Dove is, very sensibly, called Dove Dale.

Cross the river by the ancient packhorse bridge (Viator Bridge) and follow the "public footpath to Dove Dale". The well-made path keeps close to the pleasantly gurgling and sparkling river, home to numbers of busy mallard, and the valley side scenery becomes ever more spectacular. Of particular note are great rock faces, including Ravens Tor. The huge caverns of Dove Holes are worth a stop for exploration, obligatory if there are children in the party. The area by the caverns is quite outstanding scenically, with the jumbled rock accompanied by the blazing yellow of the gorse and the daffodils in April.

A little further, turn right to cross the river by the footbridge close to the Ilam Rock pinnacle, then right again along the path on the far side of the river, soon turning left into Hall Dale. This dale is a "dry" dale, so typical of the limestone country and, compared with Dove Dale, is quiet and almost remote. The path is at first steep and stony, but the gradient eases and the walking on grass towards the hamlet of Stanshope is excellent. As the dale is left, the path crosses fields from stile to stile, with yellow arrows on posts.

At Stanshope turn left at an unsurfaced lane, right at the public road, and right again along a road with a cul de sac sign, passing Church Farm and Grove Farm in quick succession. The delightful stony lane descends towards Dale Bottom, with Alstonefield church in view across the dale.

Cross the road in the bottom to a stile almost opposite and climb the steep bank on a well-worn grassy/muddy path. Turn left at the angle of a wall and head for the church. Bend left to keep close to a

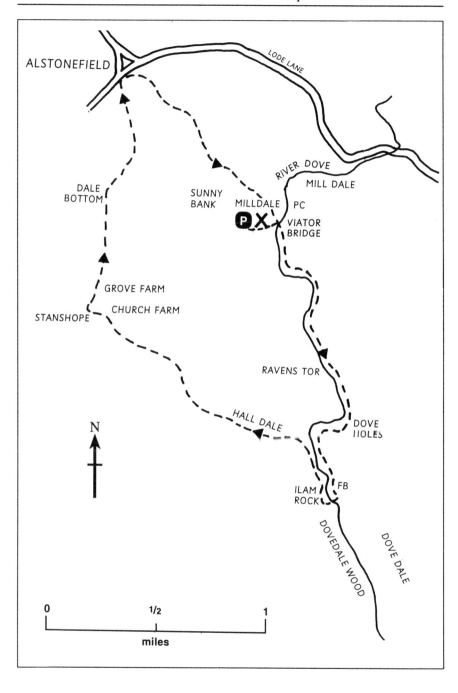

stone wall along the edge of a large field, leaving the field at the top left corner, and follow the lane ahead into Alstonefield. At the road turn right, then immediately right again, then fork right by the telephone box to reach the tea room at the post office.

Emerging from the tea shop, turn left to head towards the parish church. By the far end of the churchyard turn right at a stile by a gate, with an arrow. Follow a just visible track across the field to a stile and signpost at the far end. Bear a little left and continue over another stile before descending steeply on grass to return to Milldale village. Turn right, up the road for a short distance to the car park.

23. Hartington, Beresford Dale and Wolfscote Dale

Length:	6¾ miles.
Summary:	Beresford Dale, Wolfscote Dale and Biggin Dale combine to give a wonderful circuit predominantly following dale bottom footpaths, but with a plateau-level last section returning to Hartington. Apart from a very short distance close to the village, the paths are good and well-marked throughout.
Car Parking:	Spaces in the centre of the village or small public car park close to centre. Grid reference: 128604.
Map:	Ordnance Survey Outdoor Leisure No. 24, Peak District, White Peak area, 1:25000.

The Tea Shop

Of the several possible refreshment places in the centre of Hartington, we chose the attractive Beresford Tea Room, finding the decor good, the service pleasant, and the matching crockery of good design. With a well-varied menu of light meals and beverages at reasonable prices, what more could one ask?

Scones were accompanied by butter and jam in generous quantity, home-made cakes were excellent, and a pot of tea for two yielded six full cups.

Open seven days each week all the year 10.30 to 5pm but it is advisable to check as this cafe certainly closed on a wet, quiet, day at 4.45pm- disappointing to do the walk and then not to be able to enjoy the tea! Tel. 01298 84418.

Description

Beresford Dale and Wolfscote Dale are just two of the several names applied to different parts of the delightful valley of the River Dove. Oddly, although the Wolfscote section immediately follows the Beresford section, they are quite different in character. Both are winding but, whereas Beresford Dale is well-wooded, with exposed limestone cliffs, Wolfscote is much more open, with far less trees and great patches of scree on the steep valley sides. The river has been improved for fishing by the construction of many weirs.

At the entrance to Beresford Dale, on the right behind trees, is Charles Cotton's fishing lodge, a small building erected in 1674 as a base for his local fishing exploits with his friend Isaak Walton (of "Compleat Angler" fame). Here, they would no doubt relax convivially whilst discussing the odd one that got away from these two most assiduous anglers. Cotton, owner of the nearby Beresford Hall, was also noted for his ability to avoid creditors although eventually the estate had to be sold.

Hartington Hall

Biggin Dale is a "dry" dale, noted for the comparatively unusual great patches of gorse, blazing yellow in the spring.

Hartington is a substantial village, well spread out in the middle, where a duck pond faces a small shop selling locally made cheese. The church is mainly 14th century, with some fragments of more ancient stones to be found. Hartington Hall, a fine gabled building, long used as a youth hostel, was constructed in the 16th century and restored in the 19th.

The Walk

Leave the village centre along the road towards Hulme End, passing the Charles Cotton Hotel. In a few yards, on the left, are the public conveniences. Turn left here, noting the fine old footpath sign in front of the Gentlemen's. Go through the small gate behind the building, to head for Beresford Dale along a well-made rising foot-path. Cross a little lane and continue across the fields, occasional posts with arrows confirming the obvious route.

As woodland is approached look out for a small stone building to the right behind trees. This is the fishing house mentioned above.

The excellent path now follows the River Dove along Beresford Dale, a most attractive part of the Peak District's most famous valley, with exposed limestone, varied woodland, and dippers and wagtails keeping company with the ubiquitous mallard. At "the pike in the pool", a jutting finger of rock rises abruptly from the water.

The river is crossed twice on bridges. After the second bridge, the path crosses a rather muddy meadow to continue down Wolfscote Dale, owned by the National Trust. This dale is much less wooded than Beresford Dale, the sides being scarred by large patches of scree.

The junction with Biggin Dale is reached by a wall with stile. Do not go over the stile; turn left for a muddy start up Biggin Dale. This is a dry dale, like Wolfscote Dale with a great deal of scree, but with the rather unusual feature of large patches of gorse, blazing yellow in the spring. The path is natural but is mostly good, with just the

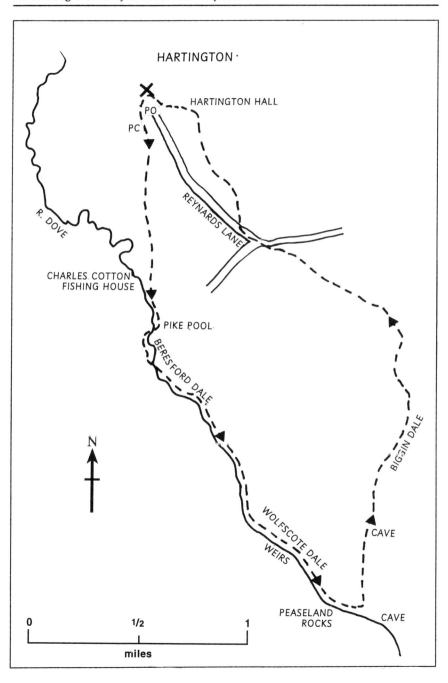

HARTINGTON ·

HARTINGTON HALL

PO

PC

R. DOVE

REYNARDS LANE

CHARLES. COTTON
FISHING HOUSE

PIKE POOL·

BERESFORD DALE

N

BIGGIN DALE

WOLFSCOTE DALE

WEIRS

CAVE

PEASELAND
ROCKS

CAVE

0   1/2   1
miles

odd muddy or stony section. The upper part of the dale is an English Nature National Nature Reserve.

At a meeting of paths near a dew-pond, with signpost, turn left to follow "Hartington". At a further signpost, turn left again to rise to a gate and stile giving access to a grassy lane between stone walls. Continue to a public road, surfaced under its usual covering of mud, and go straight ahead for 300 yards. Surmount an awkward stile on the right, signposted "Hartington" (or keep to the road if you don't like the look of the stile).

From the stile, angle a little to the right to pass through gaps in stone walls, the route being just visible on the ground. On reaching a rough farm lane turn left towards Hartington. Turn left at the public road opposite Hartington Hall to return to the village centre.

24. Longnor and Earl Sterndale

Length:	4¼ miles.
Summary:	A circuit which includes two high-lying villages and the broad valley of the upper River Dove which separates them. There is some ascent in each half of the route, but this is not too strenuous and is without difficulty underfoot.
Car Parking:	In Earl Sterndale village. Grid reference: 091670
Map:	Ordnance Survey Outdoor Leisure No. 24, Peak District, White Peak area, 1:25000.

The Tea Shop

Situated in the former Market Hall at Longnor, the coffee shop at the Craft Centre is an interesting enterprise. The tables for customers and the furniture and craft works for sale are pleasantly mixed together in this high ceilinged building. An attractive solid wooden staircase leads to a gallery with a display of original paintings. Formerly, the centre marketed only the work of one family, but now sells a range of good quality articles by craftsmen living and working in and around the Peak District.

Scones, cakes and fruit bread are all made on the premises, with the baking aroma tempting the appetite. Tea and coffee is served by the pot or in individual mugs, crockery is of a pleasant design, and there are fresh flowers on the tables. The centre is open from 10am to 5pm daily; weekends only during January and February. Tel. 01298 83587.

Description

Longnor has been described as a miniature market town. With square, four inns, a few cobbled alleyways among the clustered

stone buildings, and more than one shop, it still does its best to live up to this rather flattering description, despite a population which makes it very firmly a village. Its former importance was largely as a result of the intersection here of 18th century turnpike roads, crossing the extensive moorland. The village is perched on a ridge separating the valleys of the upper Dove and the upper Manifold.

Earl Sterndale has never had any such pretensions. The quaintly named and signed Quiet Woman Inn, the Victorian church, and a small post office/stores on the edge of the village constitute the total of the facilities of this modest community.

The upper reaches of the River Dove, in flat farmland between the hills, give no hint of the drama and the beauty to come when this famous river cuts deep into the limestone only a few miles downstream. Close to the source, however, are two of the most shapely hills in the whole district, Chrome Hill and Parkhouse Hill, sharp peaks showing most impressively from much of the route of this walk.

Between the two hills is Dowel Dale; a diversion of ½ mile along the minor road in this dale leads to a cave used by stone age hunter/gatherers. Ten skeletons were unearthed during excavations.

The Walk

At the front of the Quiet Woman, a notice advises walkers of the footpath behind the inn. Go to the right, between the inn and a garage and then through a smallholding area behind the inn, to a stile. Keep to the left of the rising field beyond, making for a stile in the top corner, followed by another, rather awkward, stile.

The path now bends left on to a ridge with good views before descending diagonally down the hillside. The path, stony in part, is just visible on the ground. Go over the stile in the wall at the bottom, aiming straight for the building ahead, where a gateway gives access to a farm roadway.

Turn left along this roadway. The impressive hill above to the left is Wheeldon. After passing Underhill Farm, the track bends to the left. Turn right here to take the signposted bridleway to "Longnor 1". The inviting grassy route heads towards a long ridge, crossing the River Dove by a footbridge – Beggar's Bridge. The same line is continued up a rising meadow and then towards a solitary farm building..

From this building, a farm roadway climbs steadily up the scarp towards Top o'th'Edge on the fringe of Longnor. Turn left, then keep right to reach the village centre, with the craft gallery/tea shop in the central square.

From the tea shop turn right and then right again to take the main Buxton road, past the Horseshoe Inn. Turn right at Church Street and then left immediately into a rising, surfaced, lane. In 100 yards ascend steps in the bank on the right, go over a stile and cross the garden at the rear of a pair of semi-detached bungalows. Go over another stile and cross a field to a stile over the wall on the far side.

Descend the scarp through light woodland. Chrome Hill and Parkhouse Hill make a fine sight ahead, having more claim to the "peak" title than almost anything else in the district. Join a farm roadway in the bottom, turning left to a gate with squeezer stile and signpost. Follow the roadway for only a short distance, then angle right to pass a dwelling about 30 yards to its right through a wide break in a wall. Stay close to the hedge for 100 yards to a stile on the right, pass another house and follow its driveway over a stile/cattle grid.

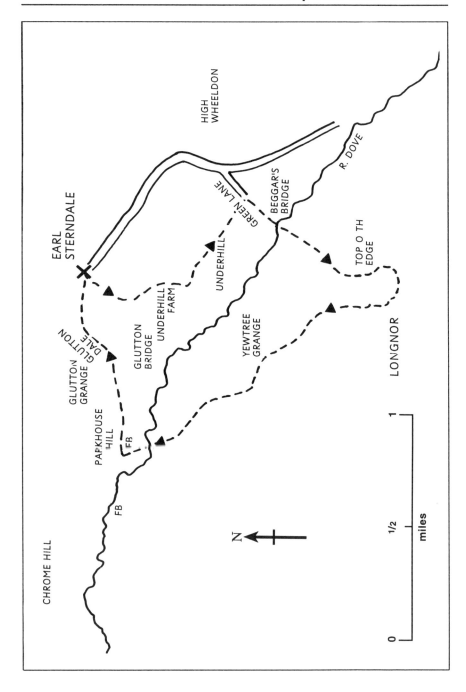

HIGH WHEELDON

R. DOVE

GREEN LANE

BEGGAR'S BRIDGE

EARL STERNDALE

UNDERHILL

TOP O TH EDGE

GLUTTON DALE

UNDERHILL FARM

GLUTTON BRIDGE

YEWTREE GRANGE

LONGNOR

GLUTTON GRANGE

PARKHOUSE HILL

FB

FB

CHROME HILL

N

1   1/2   0
        miles

Parkhouse Hill and Chrome Hill, near Longnor

Head up the roadway past Yew Tree Grange Farm to the public road. Turn right for a little more than 300 yards, then left along a lane with a footpath sign. As the lane dips to the right to a house, go straight ahead to a stile. On reaching a large meadow, angle to the right to descend to a just visible footbridge over the River Dove. Pass an unsightly disturbed area of ground and join a very minor road.

Turn right and, in a short distance, angle up to the left, making for a farm gate and stile. Note the large and crude sign above which discourages any would-be climbers of Parkhouse Hill. The track is just visible on the grass as it forks right to descend over more stiles to reach the public road.

Go straight across the road and angle left to a stile at the top of the small field and follow the path as it climbs over the shoulder of Hitter Hill to a stile over the wall at the top. Continue much the same line to head for Earl Sterndale church, passing the end of a stone wall before reaching a stile/farm gate and the road, close to the Quiet Woman.

25. The Roaches

Length:	7 miles
Summary:	One of the more demanding walks in the book, with ascent to over 1600 feet and a good deal of path which is rough underfoot. The proximity to striking rock formations and the extensive views make the effort very worthwhile.
Car Parking:	Roadside spaces in marked bays within the area which is restricted for the local park and ride scheme at weekends. Grid reference: 005622.
Map:	Ordnance Survey Outdoor Leisure No. 24, Peak District, White Peak area, 1:25000.

The Tea Shop

A delicious aroma of bacon and egg, with the comforting warmth from a wood burning stove greets the visitor to Paddock Farm where, in addition to cream or plain teas or just a cup of tea or coffee, truly genuine farmhouse breakfasts, including Staffordshire oatcakes, and "hiker's lunches" can be enjoyed. The complete menu of home-made food, is available throughout the day.

The room is typical of an old farmhouse, with corner cupboard, dresser, and Victorian portraits adorning the walls, whilst the outside seating commands fine views over the adjacent countryside. Service is pleasant and the opening hours are from 9am to 7pm every day except Christmas Day. Tel. 01538 300345.

Description

The main scarp of the Roaches, rising sharply more than 1000 feet from the Cheshire Plain, together with its offshoots Hen Cloud and Ramshaw Rocks, ranks very highly in any assessment of Peak

Hen Cloud from Paddock Farm

District scenery. On this western fringe the outcropping gritstone has a more complex and interesting form than the continuous line of "edges" at the eastern extremity of the district. Complicated folding has produced a series of ridges and basins with some remarkable rock pinnacles and towers, those of Ramshaw Rocks in particular thrusting outwards at a uniform angle. There are many esteemed and much used climbing routes on the crag faces.

This walk includes the full length of the main Roaches ridge, with the return in part along a very minor road on the east side of the ridge, with extensive views over Goldsitch Moss, a coal bearing basin overlying successive layers of gritstone and sandstone.

The Walk

Return a few yards towards Upper Hulme and turn left to take a wide stony track rising towards the low saddle separating the bulk of the Roaches (derived from the French "rochers" – rocks) from Hen Cloud ("clud"- ancient Celtic for peak). Most of the walk lies within the Roaches Estate, owned by the Peak National Park Authority.

The sharply defiant thrust of the peak of Hen Cloud is well seen from this track, as indeed from a wide area to the south, west and north. To the left is a curiously sited house, built almost under the cliffs which provide such a popular playground for rock climbers.

At a junction of footpaths turn sharp left to climb fairly steeply up the southern end of the Roaches scarp. This popular path, part of the Staffordshire Moorlands Way, has had some work carried out to repair erosion damage. The path levels to wind most attractively between the foot of the gritstone crags and the top edge of a coniferous plantation. At a little signpost turn sharp right to rise to the top of the scarp, now permitting long views to the east.

The way now continues unmistakably along this crest for about two miles. The views are superb, encompassing a wide expanse of the Staffordshire moorland country, with the attractive Tittesworth reservoir prominent. Part way along, the two step configuration of the Roaches edge is obvious as the "Five Clouds" are seen from above as nothing more than gentle rounded hummocks. A trig point marks

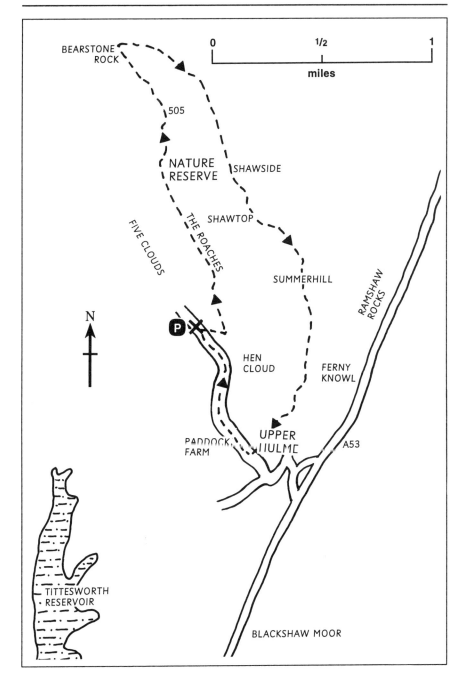

the summit at 505m (1658ft.), following which a descent is made past huge rocks of fantastic shape to join an unfenced moorland road at Roach End.

Turn right to continue along the road, still part of the Staffordshire Moorland Way, for 1⅓ miles. This is one of the very few roads which I can unreservedly recommend for walkers. There is very little traffic and the views embrace great expanses of moorland, with some obviously impoverished marginal farming to vary the landscape. The quiet walker will be rewarded by the sight and sound of moorland birds.

100 yards after a cattle grid turn right at a public footpath signpost to follow a rough farm roadway. At the approach to Shaw Top, turn left over a stile, then right, to pass close to the farm boundary fence, over some wet ground. The path soon becomes obvious, leading to another stile. Follow the arrows on posts to reach a farm access roadway. Go straight across this roadway to a second, similar, roadway in a few yards. Turn right towards a small farm.

Go through the farm gate, pass the house, and exit by another gate in the bottom right corner. Bear a little left to a stile at the far edge of the field, turn right to traverse some boggy ground, aiming for the depression ahead. The path becomes clearer on the ground as a footbridge is approached. Cross, and continue in the same direction, with a glimpse of Upper Hulme hamlet.

Cross the stream to reach a stile, go straight ahead to another stile, and carry on alongside a fence and ruined wall. Below, to the left is the rather industrial looking agricultural complex of Ferry Knoll. A farm track is followed across grazing land, bending left then right to descend to a farm access roadway.

Turn left to follow this lane as it terraces nicely around the southern flank of Hen Cloud. Join the public road by a farm gate, turning right to reach the Roaches Tea Room at Paddock Farm.

After refreshment, the last lap is along the road for about ¾ mile to the car park, with ample time and opportunity to admire again the fine profile of Hen Cloud.

26. Wildboarclough and Shutlingsloe

Length:	3½ miles.
Summary:	The ascent of Shutlingsloe (1659 feet), an attractive rocky peak and a good viewpoint, plus a ramble around Wildboarclough itself are combined in this walk. A little steep and rocky underfoot on the last section of Shutlingsloe, but no real difficulty.
Car Parking:	Official car park near Clough House, nearly one mile north of Wildboarclough. Grid reference: 987698.
Map:	Ordnance Survey Outdoor Leisure No. 24, Peak District, White Peak area. 1:25000.

The Tea Shop

The Brookside restaurant at Wildboarclough is just the place for a real old-fashioned high tea: plaice, gammon, sausage, egg, etc., all served with good chips, tea and bread and butter. Nicely presented salads offer a lighter alternative for the more calorie conscious, whilst light refreshments such as afternoon teas and the usual tea or coffee with cakes are, of course, also available.

The proprietress, Mrs. Higson, who was born here, told us that her grandmother started the cafe in this former farm building more than 40 years ago. It is now pleasantly furnished and welcomes walkers, subject only to the leaving of muddy boots in the porch.

The only disadvantage is that the opening hours are somewhat restricted: 12 noon to 5.30pm on Wednesdays, Saturdays, Sundays, and Bank Holiday Mondays. (Easter to mid September) and the same hours but on Saturdays and Sundays only during the remainder of the year. Tel. 01260 227632

Brookside cafe, Wildboarclough

Description

Shutlingsloe has, with great exaggeration, been referred to as "the Matterhorn of the Peak District". It is, nevertheless, one of the most shapely peaks in the district, with views which include the Jodrell Bank telescope end extend to the Mersey Plain. The ascent is quite straightforward.

It might come as a surprise to learn that Wildboarclough, in its remote sylvan setting, was, in fact, an early 19th century industrial community. Crag Works was constructed here by George Palfreyman in about 1800 as a calico printing factory, nearby Crag Hall being built at the same time as his residence. The name Crag was taken from two farmsteads in the ancient township of Wildboarclough.

Apart from the necessity of having abundant supplies of soft water, both for processing and for powering the water wheel, the chosen location appeared to have few advantages, being distant from similar industries and with difficult communications, particularly in winter. Stanley Pool was created as a reservoir above the works, fed by a conduit from a weir on the Clough Brook, well upstream at Clough House Farm. Part of the works was four stories tall; one wing remains, now known as the Old Post Office. Several rows of cottages, two of which remain, were built to house the workers, with a chapel and a school added to this thriving little community.

Before the middle of the century calico printing gave way to carpet printing, but only for a few years. The works closed in 1860, following which the industrial community died.

St. Saviour's church, consecrated in 1909, was built on the site of the former works dye house, re-using much of the stone of the earlier building. Before that time, Wildboarclough was part of the huge parish of Prestbury and was very distant from the parish church. From 1673, a church built at Macclesfield Forest, within the Prestbury parish, somewhat eased the travelling problems of parishioners but was still so remote that a schoolroom at the works was licensed for Anglican services, but not for marriages or burials, from 1853 until 1909. The Methodist chapel was sited near what is now the west gate of St. Saviour's church, from 1790 to 1852.

The Walk

Start along the road towards Wildboarclough. Turn right in a short distance at a sign "Langley via Shutlingsloe" to take an excellent path terracing above the road and soon along the top edge of a plantation.

At a farm gate, with adjacent cattle grid, turn sharp right to begin the ascent proper on a farm roadway. Well short of the farm, turn left at a signpost. The waymarked route to the summit is never in doubt; most of the way is easy underfoot, but the last section is steep and stony.

The basically level summit, with trig. point, commands a wonderful range of views, identification being aided by a memorial plaque which doubles as a viewing table. Prominent to the south is the end of the high ridge of the Roaches.

To return from the peak, either retrace the outward route or, for a more gentle initial descent, head along the paved path towards Langley, turning right in a short distance on a path which circles back to re-join the outward route at a prominent signpost.

From the cattle grid, turn right along a lane. The lake which was the reservoir constructed to supply water to Crag Mill is just visible through the trees. Join the public road and turn right, passing the Crag Inn. The tea shop (Brookside restaurant) is about ½ mile distant.

Return along the road to Wildboarclough and turn right to cross the bridge over the Clough Brook, where a plaque records the disastrous flood of 1989. On the left is the former mill house, then another elegant building, a part of the mill which was later used as the village post office. The church, on the knoll, is early 19th century but its construction re-used local materials, largely taken from a former dye-house on the same site. A little track up the bank behind the church permits a close view of the old reservoir, now an attractive lake.

Continue along the lane beside the church, passing a terrace of mill cottages before re-joining the road and returning to the car park.

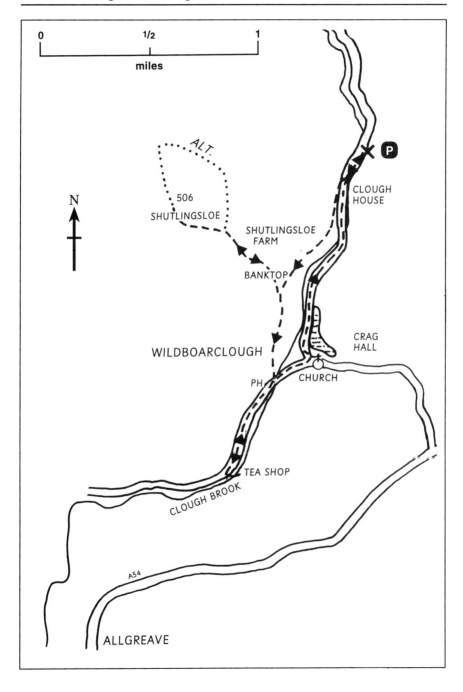

MORE TEA SHOP WALKS:

Lake District • Lancashire • Cheshire • Cotswolds
Great value at £6.95!

MORE COUNTRY WALKS:

LAKELAND ROCKY RAMBLES: Geology beneath your feet – Bryan Lynas *(£9.95)*

LAKELAND WALKING, ON THE LEVEL – Norman Buckley *(£6.95)*

MOSTLY DOWNHILL: LEISURELY WALKS, LAKE DISTRICT – Alan Pears *(£6.95)*

100 LAKE DISTRICT HILL WALKS – Gordon Brown *(£7.95)*

PUB WALKS IN THE LAKE DISTRICT – Neil Coates *(£6.95)*

PUB WALKS IN THE YORKSHIRE DALES – Clive Price *(£6.95)*

PUB WALKS ON THE NORTH YORK MOORS & COAST – Stephen Rickerby *(£6.95)*

PUB WALKS IN THE YORKSHIRE WOLDS – Tony Whittaker *(£6.95)*

BEST PUB WALKS IN & AROUND SHEFFIELD – Clive Price *(£6.95)*

SOUTH YORKSHIRE WALKS – Martin Smith *(£6.95)*

YORKSHIRE DALES WALKING: ON THE LEVEL – Norman Buckley *(£6.95)*

MOSTLY DOWNHILL IN THE PEAK DISTRICT – Clive Price *(£6.95)*
(two volumes, White Peak & Dark Peak)

DISCOVERY WALKS IN DERBYSHIRE - Paul & Sandra Biggs *(£6.95)*

EAST CHESHIRE WALKS – Graham Beech *(£6.95)*

WEST CHESHIRE WALKS – Jen Darling *(£5.95)*

WALKS IN MYSTERIOUS WALES – Laurence Main *(£6.95)*

PUB WALKS IN SNOWDONIA – Laurence Main *(£6.95)*

RAMBLES AROUND MANCHESTER – Mike Cresswell *(£5.95)*

WEST PENNINE WALKS – Mike Cresswell *(£5.95)*

All of our books are available from your local bookshop. In case of difficulty, or to obtain our complete catalogue, please contact:

Sigma Leisure, 1 South Oak Lane, Wilmslow, Cheshire SK9 6AR
Phone: 01625 – 531035   Fax: 01625 – 536800

ACCESS and VISA orders welcome – call our friendly sales staff or use our 24 hour Answerphone service! Most orders are despatched on the day we receive your order – you could be enjoying our books in just a couple of days. Please add £2 p&p to all orders.